WILL THE REAL JOHN CALLAHAN PLEASE STAND UP?

Freaks of Nature

What Kind of God Would Allow a Thing like This to Happen?!!

The King of Things and the Cranberry Clown

The Night, They Say, Was Made for Love

Do What He Says! He's Crazy!

Digesting the Child Within

Do Not Disturb Any Further

Don't Worry, He Won't Get Far on Foot

LURID REVELATIONS · SHOCKING REJECTIONS · IRATE LETTERS

WILLIAM MORROW AND COMPANY, INC.

NEW YORK

WILL THE REAL JOHN CALLAHAN PLEASE STAND UP?

A QUASI MEMOIR

JoHn CALLaHan

INTRODUCTION BY ROBIN WILLIAMS

It is the policy of William Morrow and Company, Inc., and its
imprints and affiliates, recognizing the importance of preserving
what has been written, to print the books we publish
on acid-free paper, and we exert our best efforts to that end.

Library of Congress Cataloging-in-Publication Data

Callahan, John, 1951–
Will the real John Callahan please stand up?—a quasi memoir:
lurid revelations, shocking rejections, irate letters / John Callahan;
introduction by Robin Williams.—1st ed.
p.   cm.
ISBN 0-688-13339-8 (paper-over-boards)
1. Callahan, John, 1951– . 2. Cartoonists—United States—
Biography. I Title.
NC1429.C23A2   1998
741.5'092   97-33327
[B]—DC21   CIP

Printed in the United States of America

First Edition

1 2 3 4 5 6 7 8 9 10

BOOK DESIGN BY JO ANNE METSCH

www.williammorrow.com

For Robin Williams,
who has been such an inspiration
and who paid for my decaf at
Joe's Bar in San Francisco

ACKNOWLEDGMENTS

First and foremost, I want to thank Deborah Levin and Elmer Luke.
Thanks too to Marlos DePaula, Francine Rose, and Dale Mills.

John Callahan has been called a sick and twisted individual. Not true! First of all, he's not sick; he's a perfectly healthy quadriplegic. And second, he has attendants who straighten him out in the event he ever gets twisted. But does Callahan have a sick, twisted sense of humor? . . . Well, come to think of it, yeah, he does. Emphasis on the word humor.

Not everybody, it seems, shares Callahan's sense of humor. He's an Irishman who knows how to make you laugh by getting your Irish up. For instance, check out the hilariously outrageous cartoons involving a naked nun or the polio mimes. With cartoons like those, Callahan has a knack for causing pious folks to froth at the mouth, spew bile, and curse him as the Demon of Bad Taste. He has that sort of charming effect on people. He can also get people like me rolling on the floor with laughter (which is, actually, one of the only physical actions he and I can do together).

Callahan's cartoons will make some of his readers all piss and vinegar. But one man's piss and vinegar is another man's sweet and sour. And if that thought isn't bizarre enough for you, read on.

ROBIN WILLIAMS

WILL THE REAL JOHN CALLAHAN PLEASE STAND UP?

A PREFACE

When I was a child, I noticed that my grandfather pulled his pants up very high after using the bathroom. The memory of this haunted me throughout my life. Many months ago I finally sat down and wrote out my thoughts about it. As I continued to write, it developed into a bit of a story. I rather liked it. Also, it helped me release some of the old demons that had been plaguing me. I felt a sense of relief I'd never known. A kind of freedom, a catharsis, in knowing that my grandfather's bathroom habits no longer had any power over me.

Now it was no longer just my secret. I showed the story to some of my friends. They seemed to find it, as I'd hoped, curiously dark and compelling, or so they said. I wouldn't put it past those pricks to cruelly mislead me as to the viability of my first attempt at memoir.

Nevertheless, I continued to put pen to paper about more and more of the odd remembrances of my short but paralyzed life. It was hard work and scary, but oddly satisfying. Most of all, it was a welcome departure from the constrictive parameters of cartooning.

I put the stories in a drawer and forgot about them. Several months ago, my publisher called and announced it was time for a new book. I asked what kind of book they wanted. "Your choice" was the reply. I thought about it for a few weeks. "My choice?"

More time passed and my confusion only deepened. Then one day, I picked up a copy of the *Los Angeles Times,* and there on page A12 of the Metro section was an angry letter to the editor concerning one of my cartoons. It read: ". . . and so with all the funny cartoonists in this world to choose from, why must you continue to publish the poorly drawn and unfunny cartoons of John Callahan?"

This was the answer! Why not publish, alongside some lurid revelations, a collection of the best (or the worst) of the letters to the editor I'd received for the past ten years? No cartoonist on earth had received more disgruntled letters than I.

I set about organizing the project immediately. This could be fun. My mind began to race. What about those drawings of mine I'd saved from grade school? What about those rejected strip ideas that had laid me so low at the beginning of my career . . . and the K-Man strip that I'm still toying with for possible syndication? I'd include them all!

I bet there were a few people, at least, who'd be interested in the letters received from President Clinton and from Richard Pryor, or in the transcript from the O.J. trial, when Judge Ito mentioned my name in court, or the letters between the judge and me that followed.

I organized little sorting parties with my friends during which they tore into the four corners of the house, searching for perfect, rejected old-time cartoons. My friend Laura made me promise to include the account of my meeting Bob Dylan, when I shamed myself hideously and beyond comprehension. My friends said, "We all know that you've humiliated yourself in Portland. Now tell the world!"

"Those pricks!" I thought. But I took their advice, and here's the book. I hope you like it.

I didn't want to be accused of predictability, so I've gone with my mental flow and I've placed cartoons here and there, some out of context and chronology, to keep you awake. Pictures are supposed to stimulate idle minds, and don't they say a cartoon is worth a thousand words anyway? Don't complain to me if the order of the book doesn't make sense, because that's how I live each day.

J.C.
Portland, Oregon

BEGINNINGS

hese are the earliest Callahan cartoons that have survived. Everything else was burned up in a horrible fire that was started by a careless poor white trash cousin of mine.

CALLAHAN (1ˢᵗ cartoon) age 9

URETHRA FrankLiN!

JOHNNY C

CALLAHAN   age 9

FRank SNOTra

JOHNNie

GRANDPA OTTO

There's something that haunts me. Thirty years beyond, and it still haunts me. And it seems such a silly thing to be haunted about! I can't believe I'd even mention it, but here goes. I keep having this memory of my grandpa. Grandpa Otto. I don't even recall that much about him—he must have been about ninety-eight when I was born. But what I remember about him concerns his pants.

Grandpa Otto always pulled his pants up really high after he was finished using the bathroom. I suppose that isn't so unusual. Many men emerge from the bathroom with their pants pulled a bit higher than when they went into the bathroom.

But the degree to which Grandpa Otto did this is the point of my disorientation. Grandpa Otto was, for all practical purposes, an egg-shaped man. Much like the famed Humpty-Dumpty. He had thin arms and legs hinging from a huge bloated torso. At most times, Grandpa Otto necessarily circumvented the belt line, the very apex of his egglike torso. Not unlike the equator around the direct center of the world. He did not take the "plumber's way out" by letting his pants hang far below and beneath his protruding pot. He pulled his pants around right up to the point that most accentuated the impertinent porkiness of his paunch.

But when the man emerged from the wafting world of the porcelain throne room, his pants were always a full ten to twelve inches above what might be the normal level. Out into the hallway the ancient man would stride, with a look of relief brightening his wrinkled face, a youthful lightness in his step—and his pants pulled up almost to the level of his nipples. Everyone would smirk as he paraded around the living room calling each of us guys "buckeroo" and exhorting the womenfolk to keep up the activity in the kitchen—which would, of course, contribute eventually to his need for another trip to the WC.

"Why does Grandpa Otto always pull his pants up too high after he gets done going poo-poo?"

"Hush!" my mother would whisper. But there was as always a twinkle in her eye as she looked up.

I remember sitting on the floor as a child, watching him walk about with his pants so very high. I remember thinking that his pants were raised as a tribute to the heroic passage of the little fecal soldiers so recently flushed and forgotten down the cold, cold crapper.

My father felt that Grandpa Otto was actually increasing the height of his pants over time. "Pretty soon he'll have to unzip his zipper in order to talk!"

All in all, I seem to have stopped those unsettling memories of my now long-dead grandfather. But sometimes at night I see him looming before me with his pants pulled high and his white socks gleaming. "Pull 'em high, boy!" he'd shout. "It's your legacy!"

I wake up screaming, "No! No! I won't pull them high! I won't! I won't!" And back I sink into the pillow, sweating and weeping.

NUNS, WONDERFUL NUNS

I don't know why this nun collection is so roundly rejected. I still think that a group of sisters found out about it and blocked it from being published by threatening to take rulers and smash the knuckles of any editor who attempted to publish it.

(front view of face)

NUN RIDING UNICYCLE

NUN WITH SPEAR
THROUGH HEAD
(unable to get through
revolving door.)

HIT NUN

ME WITH NUN
(1957)

NUN IN SUMMER
(wearing HAWAIIAN Habit)

(NONE NUNS)

PUNK NUN

NUN (MODERN) CHOOSING NOT TO WEAR HABIT.

NUN BANISHED TO STREET

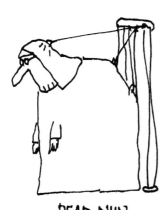

DEAD NUN
(propped up)

celibate's leap

SUICIDAL NUNS

BIG FOOT

When my brother and I were preschoolers, my family moved from Portland, Oregon, to the small town of The Dalles, Oregon. Everyone hated it, especially my mother, who complained constantly of the ever-present photos of Indians fishing, which were placed in every store, bank, and beauty shop. It was a nice quiet place to raise kids, but God help you if you were a homosexual or a Negro.

When I entered the eighth grade, I met Joe Evans, who lived on a farm several miles outside of town. As we became better friends, I spent more and more time on the farm with Joe. We spent many happy hours running through the woods, shooting .22s, and building rafts by the creek. Smokey and Blackie were Joe's two dogs, and they followed us everywhere. We usually returned to the farmhouse in the late afternoon and were met by Joe's mother and father and the six other children, who were preparing for dinner. At night, Joe and I slept in the bunkhouse with Joe's older brothers. We listened to the yelp of the coyotes high above us where the timberline began. It was a wild, haunting feeling and completely different from the regimented suburban life at my parents' house in town.

One night I awoke to hear scratching, and Smokey and Blackie barking at the back door of the farmhouse. Joe whispered to me, "That's unusual; those dogs hate being in the house." I heard the door shut behind them as Mrs. Evans let them in.

I drifted back to sleep after a few moments of uneasiness. I tossed and turned throughout the night and awoke to hear excited voices outside the bunkhouse.

I pulled my boots on, and I leapt outside. There was a newly fallen blanket of snow covering everything within sight. I could hear the voices of Mr. and Mrs. Evans and a couple of the boys down near the barn. As I rounded the corner of the old pump shed, I could see them all standing near the corral. There was something strange about their voices, and why were two sheriff's deputies with them? Joe intercepted me halfway down the path, breathless, eyes wide as saucers. "Where have you been? . . . What did you hear? . . . Have you seen the tracks? . . ."

"What tracks?!" I screamed.

Joe grabbed my sleeve and ran me down to the assembled group. An awful stench hovered in the air. I could hear Mrs. Evans stammering to the officer, "I thought it was unusual that the dogs were so frightened last night. They've never wanted in the house before. And this morning when I was carrying the trash down to the dump, they wouldn't leave my side. That's when I first saw the tracks."

I glanced over my left shoulder to where she was pointing and saw a third deputy taking pictures of something in the snow about sixty feet downhill from us near the dump. "My God, Officer, what's been here?" she said.

My heart was pounding as my imagination ran wild. Another car pulled up, and two men in overcoats emerged from it.

That's all I remember of the incident, because the men in overcoats hustled us back into the house where we were told to stay.

All the adults remained secretive about what went on out there, and to this day I still don't know what conclusion was arrived at.

The bad luck that I had with pets doesn't nearly compare with the bad luck I had in getting this piece published.

MY PETS
by Callahan

my first pet was a $1.00 goldfish.

But it jumped out of the bowl, and I found him stiff and dead one morning...

when I was 9 my mother let me have a guinea pig...

... I never knew about those special tube-water bottles so my guinea pig became dehydrated. But I just thought he was being lethargic...

I knew it was wrong, but I tried to perk him up by jabbing him with a sharp pencil...

my mother said the situation was hopeless, and that I should put him out of his misery. So I took him out to the backyard and killed him with a croquet mallet...

I buried him behind the garage although I felt guilty about it.. I kept digging him up to see how much he'd decomposed...

my turtle dried up in the sunlight of the window sill ...

Next, I got a turtle. Reddy Harris had some turtles, too, and we raced them.

Next, I received a dog for my 11th birthday. My sister accidentally tipped a chair over upon its head. This gave the dog Low self-esteem which lasted all his life.

Reddy squashed his turtle with his foot...

Sluggo did nothing but lay around on top of the picnic table and would sometimes nip at the kids, which dismayed my father...

Boy, when they start that nippin' business...

Finally, my dad took Sluggo for "a ride in the country..."

"Get in there you..."

I had no pets for several years, then I got some cats... I accidentally ran over their tails, and, upon hearing them screech, I'd quickly back up (in an attempt to move off the cat's tail), but instead I'd roll right back upon the cat tail. They would screech again and I'd pull forward—right back onto his tail, and so on...

Next, I got a bird. My girlfriend watered, or "misted" the tiny thing with a "plant mister". The bird caught a chill and kicked off in a half hour...

SSSS...

Now, I have no pets. Sometimes I dream of buying a basset hound or a snake, but never seem to get up the enthusiasm.

THE END

DYLAN

I'm trying not to panic. I'm trying to think straight.

What happened? I was cutting cookies in the living room when my wheelchair got caught up in the rug. I felt the bumping and jolting as I wound myself tighter and tighter into trouble. I jammed the joystick in rage as my circle began to slow and sluggishness overtook my motor. Round and round I bumped, as my motor burned and the rug wrapped itself tighter around my axle. Still, I would not—or could not—bring myself to give in to the forces working against me. Finally the chair lunged as I ran over the gathered bulk of rug below me, and I tipped over with a crash, thrown headlong onto my stomach. And now, here I lie, flat on my face, once again confronted with my own powerlessness and stupidity.

The hardwood floor is especially hard beneath the part of my body that I can feel. There is no one around to help me, and I don't expect my helper for another five hours. A forty-four-year-old man cutting cookies in a wheelchair. What a moron! I deserve this. Now I can lie here and recall the dumb things I've done with my life. At the very top of the list has got to be the Dylan Incident.

Bob Dylan has always been my biggest hero. As a teen, I listened to his albums day and night, teaching myself to play guitar and harmonica by copying his style. Throughout my twenties and thirties, my appreciation for his genius only increased. I could quote his song lyrics, relate his history, and interpret his dark meaning with the best of them.

Imagine my excitement when, two years ago, my friend Larry told me I was going to meet Dylan. Larry, Dylan's lifelong friend, as a favor to me, had arranged backstage passes.

The big night arrived. I was backstage with my friend Laura. I was sweating bullets and rehearsing what I was going to say when I finally came face-to-face with the legend himself. There were only a few people backstage with us. I could sense that Dylan was about to arrive as more people began trickling in and hanging around. "The assholes," I thought.

I was taking deep breaths and meditating when Laura shook my arm and whispered, "Is that him? That is him!" She pointed at a smallish, frizzy-haired man advancing through the door surrounded by a ring of large men. I strained to see— yes, it was him!

"Oh, my God," I thought, as one of his bodyguards pointed in my direction. Dylan looked where the man was pointing.

"He's looking at you!" whispered Laura.

I thought I was going to slip into an acid flashback when the Great Poet advanced within twenty feet of us. Was he going to walk right up to me? He was! He stood before me and extended his hand! The hand that strummed the guitar while he wrote "Blowin' in the Wind"!

I shook his hand. I said, "It's an honor to meet you! It's an honor to meet you!"

"You're the cartoonist, aren't you? My daughter's a big fan of your work," said Dylan.

"Well . . . yeah . . . I guess," I stuttered. He's just being nice, I thought as Dylan motioned for his daughter to come over to us.

"I love your cards," he said.

I felt myself beginning to black out as the two of them stood before me. "Oh, God, please don't let this happen," I prayed.

I was seeing stars and Dylan's face was becoming fuzzy before me. I was slipping into a faint, getting attacked by panic. In a desperate attempt to seize control of myself, of my faculties, and simultaneously to make Dylan understand I was truly a kindred spirit, I stammered, "I write songs, too."

At that moment Dylan gave me a small hug and turned and walked away, leaving me in a swirling state of starstruck numbness and self-reproach. A pounding in my temples, a queasiness, a sort of ominous voice started saying, "You idiot! You just told Bob Dylan that you write songs! You fool! The most accomplished songwriter in America—a living legend—a piece of America—the voice of a generation! Shaper of a culture, poet, prophet. Mr. Tambourine Man! And you tell him that you write songs, too! HA! You're the biggest asshole in all of history! You might as well have told the pope, 'I say prayers, too!' Or told Madonna, 'I've had intercourse, too!' "

I turned desperately to Laura. "Did you hear me tell Dylan I write songs, too? Heh, heh," I joked, hoping to put a light spin on things. But the frightened look in her eyes told me all was lost.

"Our cab is waiting. Let's go" was all she said.

Suddenly I heard the door open and my evening helper called out, "On the floor again? Let's get you back in your chair. You've wrecked this carpet!"

Yes, I'm an asshole.

THE LIGHTER SIDE OF BEING
PARALYZED FOR LIFE

ONE EVENING IN 1972, A FRIEND AND I DECIDED TO GO OUT FOR AN EVENING OF FUN...

WE ENDED THE EVENING BY DRIVING HIS VOLKSWAGEN INTO A BILLBOARD AT 90 MILES AN HOUR. (LOOKING BACK ON IT, I KIND OF WISH WE HADN'T DONE THIS.)

IN THE AMBULANCE, THE ATTENDANT ANSWERED ALL MY QUESTIONS...

IN THE INTENSIVE CARE UNIT TOO, THE DOCTOR WAS TACTFUL IN GIVING ME THE PROGNOSIS.

AT THE REHABILITATION CENTER, THERAPISTS SUPPLIED ME WITH THE LATEST IN ADAPTIVE EQUIPMENT

I EXPERIENCED THE TYPICAL DEPRESSION AND LONGED FOR THE DAYS BEFORE MY INJURY WHEN I WAS A USEFUL CONTRIBUTOR TO SOCIETY.

DURING REHABILITATION, I LEARNED MANY
USEFUL THINGS, LIKE HOW TO MOVE FROM
MY WHEELCHAIR INTO BED AND VICE
VERSA...

ONE DAY, IN A MOMENT OF DESPERATION,
I SNEAKED OUT AND WENT TO A FAITH
HEALER...

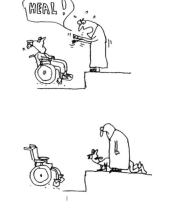

FINALLY, THE DAY CAME WHEN I WAS
RELEASED FROM THE REHAB. CENTER, AND
I WAS INTRODUCED TO THE HIGHLY
TRAINED ATTENDANT WITH WHOM I
WOULD SHARE AN APARTMENT...

THE LIVE-IN ATTENDANT AND I SPENT MANY
PRODUCTIVE HOURS TOGETHER IN OUR
APARTMENT IN LOS ANGELES.

WE HAD SPECIAL EQUIPMENT INSTALLED,
LIKE A DELUXE BATH LIFT.

AFTER A FEW MONTHS OF SLOWLY
REBUILDING MY SELF-CONFIDENCE, I
TENTATIVELY RESUMED MY SOCIAL LIFE...

...AND AFTER A WHILE BEGAN TO ACHIEVE SOME SUCCESS IN THE WORLD OF ROMANCE.

I DEVELOPED SOME NEW TECHNIQUES FOR STARTING CONVERSATIONS...

..AND AFTER A WHILE MY LIFE BECAME PRETTY NORMAL.

OF COURSE, ONE OF THE PROBLEMS OF BEING IN A WHEELCHAIR ISN'T THE FACT THAT YOU'RE IN IT, BUT THAT PEOPLE REACT TO YOU IN THE WEIRDEST WAYS...

A COUPLE OF YEARS AGO I DECIDED TO
GET SERIOUS ABOUT MY CARTOONING
AND BEGAN SELLING THEM TO LOCAL
AND THEN NATIONAL PUBLICATIONS.

*H*ERE ARE A FEW OF THEM.

was

*O*F COURSE, EVEN THOUGH I ENJOY BEING
A CARTOONIST, MY LIFE ISN'T ALWAYS A
BED OF ROSES

THE PSYCHIATRIST HELPED ME TO SEE THAT BEING IN A WHEELCHAIR ISN'T SO BAD — THERE ARE EVEN CERTAIN ADVANTAGES...

THESE DAYS I'M CONTENT TO ROAM THE STREETS OF PORTLAND LOOKING FOR NEW CARTOON IDEAS AND MEETING NEW PEOPLE. IF YOU SEE ME, SAY HELLO, AND IF YOU'D LIKE, OFFER A FEW CRITICAL COMMENTS ABOUT MY WORK...

I. You don't have to Participate in death marches.

II. If you happen to be a cartoonist, you're already sitting down.

III. If asked to dance by someone you loathe, you've a legitimate excuse not to.

Care to dance?

I'd like to, but I'm paralyzed

Best work I've seen!

Aren't you John Callahan, the brilliant Cartoonist?

Exquisite!

QUADRO

I had another bad day today. Everyone I passed on the street stared at my wheelchair. I felt terribly self-conscious, especially when a woman looked at me like I was a cross-eyed hunchback with a spear through his neck. But what took the cake was when a guy threw change in my hat when I set it down to scratch my head!

They do everything they can to make you feel like a freak—the able-bodied swine! Someday things will be different. Someday the world will be controlled by quads! That's right! Someday all quads will rise up with one collective spasm, and the world will cringe at our foot pedals.

I know you're probably laughing to yourself and thinking, "Poor bastard, Callahan, he's finally snapped from all the strain of being paralyzed for life. Quads will someday control the world indeed! That'll be a hoot! Ha! Ha!"

You can stop laughing, because it's true. How do I know it's true? Because I saw it all in a dream. Yes, I saw it all in a magnificent dream several months ago. It wasn't just an ordinary dream. No. It was one of those that speak to you, deeply move you. One that lets you know it's not just a regular frivolous dream, but more a vision, an experience!

The dream began in a familiar way. A quad is returning from a typical day of abuse by the able-bodied community. He has been stared at, patronized, architecturally locked out, pushed down stairs, and even asked if he could be used as a wheelbarrow. In his rejected state, the quad is barely able to navigate his electric wheelchair through the busy New York City sidewalks. He is bitter, almost despairing about his situation. Tears fill his down-turned eyes and he mutters angrily to himself, "Nobody has any respect for quads anymore. And after all the social progress we've made since the days of the infamous 'Jim Quad Laws,' when janitors were allowed to turn our chairs upside down on tables they were sweeping under—with us still in the chair!" "What ya' gonna do when quads won't leave?" the janitors used to laugh cruelly, as we quads hung helplessly in our upside-down chairs.

As our demoralized quad continues his path along the bustling sidewalks, he has no idea what a bizarre twist awaits him. He pulls his wheelchair to a stop as the intersection light flashes DON'T WALK. "Of course I'm not going to walk!" he thinks peevishly. Lost in his moment of personal annoyance, he does not hear the squeal of huge tires as a toxic chemical truck slams into a nearby telephone pole. Oblivious to the accident, he propels his wheelchair out into the crosswalk. Slowly he becomes aware of voices, frantic voices, shouting. He soon realizes the voices are directed at him. "Hey, you silly quad, LOOK OUT! LOOK OUT!"

As the quad turns his head in the direction their fingers are pointing, he sees that a lone toxic chemical barrel is rolling rapidly in his path. Horrified, he realizes there is nothing he can do to evade his fate. The crowd roars in horror as the barrel crashes heavily against the quad, exploding into a fiery orange ball of toxic flames.

The quad, totally immersed in flames and shrieking in blinded agony, does the worst thing a quad can do. He jams the joystick to full acceleration and careens out of control only to fan the awful flames that continue to engulf him.

Crowds gather in horror as the quad streaks through the streets, a freight train of flames. The gasps of hundreds of onlookers can be heard above the sirens of fire trucks and emergency vehicles in the echoing distance. The quad has now stopped in the middle of an intersection. The flames rise higher as he writhes in agony, flailing his charred arms. His shrieks grow wilder and more animal-like. Louder and louder grow his awful alien cries, drowning out the new screams and the sirens. Suddenly, the ground begins to tremble as the quad starts to throb, to pulsate. His charred skin begins to crack and split as an inner quad balloons into birth. Women shriek as the entity rises and grows above their eyes. The groan of grinding metal deafens them as even the wheelchair lurches into larger and larger proportions.

The crowd is caught between panic and a numbing fascination at the apparition. The resounding groans of the mutating quad shake the very buildings surrounding them. Telephone wires snap, gas mains burst, as a tortured form expands to towering proportions. Suddenly the noise and rumble subsides. The smoke and steam clears; the shrieking dies to awestruck murmurs. A horrifying specter looms above them. Standing a full five hundred feet, with blazing hair, shimmering spokes, and malevolent smile, sits a colossus of a quadriplegic.

The gargantuan gimp now cocks his flaming red head back and thunders his first words, "I AM QUADRO!"

He then spins his huge chair around, crushing some hapless bystanders beneath two-hundred-foot-high rubber wheels. The crowd watches as Quadro drives in the direction of the Twin Towers, buildings smashed beneath the wheels of his massive electric wheelchair. "Where is he going?" can be heard above the din and confusion. "It looks like he's heading straight for Gold's Gym!" And, sure enough, Quadro is bearing down fast on the colorfully appointed "mecca of muscle development."

Quadro now drives over the gymnasium, crushing the building like a matchbox. He rocks his chair back and forth over the steaming ruins in an attempt to stomp the ant-sized patrons streaming in horror from the scene. "Able-bodied swine!" he shrieks in triumph.

A crowd of quads is beginning to gather outside the rehab center across the street. "All right! All right! Go, Quadro!" scream the quads in unison, vindicated by the violence of their ethereal cousin.

Quadro, hearing their weak but hysterical screams, smiles tenderly down on them, perhaps sensing a kinship and a bond as he proceeds through the city, creating a wide swath of flattened architecture, just level enough to allow the swelling ranks of cheering quadriplegics who are falling in behind him to roll through.

Quadro, the "pied piper of paralysis," continues his glorious march through the city destroying physical fitness centers along the way. He eventually gains control of the entire world, placing his Handicapped Henchmen in positions of power. Disability rules the day! It becomes chic to be paralyzed. Everyone wants to catch the wave. People are literally diving out of windows in order to become quads! The few remaining able-bodied are looked down upon and ostracized. They are considered banal and coarse.

Quadro reigns supreme until a horde of ambulatory renegades attacks him and his infamous invalids. The fighting lasts for many days, until one of the renegades manages to shoot a hole in Quadro's leg bag, spraying urine over the surface of half the kingdom and drowning all living beings in a tsunami of urine.

CHRISTMAS WITH J.C.

grew up in a strict Irish family in The Dalles. My parents thought they couldn't have children and they adopted me. Then they had five of their own children. Dad told people that I took after his red-haired Grandma Ethel. I always felt funny about that.

One of my memories of Christmas is my mother saying, "Who will get in a big fight with Dad putting up the Christmas lights? Who's going to get in a fight with Dad nailing up the stockings?" We all got in trouble one year when we made an ornament that looked like my Dad. He had a flat-top. . . .

I was always afraid to sit on the Santa's lap at the department store. The kids said he was a wino. I remember my uncle playing Santa Claus. His beard caught on fire when he got too close to an angel candle. He was a heavy drinker. . . .

What do I want for Christmas? A van. I'd also like a green sweater for my dog, Bogey. And a new neighborhood.

"It doesn't seem like christmas without snow!"

"...AND THEN, MR. TRUMP, I'D LIKE..."

Who knows why people get so depressed during the holidays? But I do know this: Mental illness, failed relationships, amputations, broken dreams, it's all around us. People want to hide from it, especially during the holidays. So people drink, and people jump off bridges.

I draw cartoons about holiday depressions because I've been through it. I've been suicidal. . . . Suicide is an extremely tragic subject. But the truth is, we're all vulnerable. It doesn't matter if you have a healthy heart or a big bank account. The Grim Reaper can sit on your shoulder at any time.

People say, "Hey, you're the guy with those negative, cynical cartoons." And I just go, "I'm the guy." Once you've come face-to-face with the Grim Reaper, after you've gone down that road, it gives you a depth, an irreverence, and a dark sense of humor. I know a lot of people who've been through a lot of things, a lot of tragedy. What I do makes sense to them.

I'm as much a writer as an artist, though, and for me generally the gag line comes first. In my apartment the TV is on all the time, like a respirator. One day an old Errol Flynn movie was on as I worked, and a line of dialogue floated into my consciousness: "Don't be a fool, Billy!" I thought, "Boy, there's a fine old cliché."

I try to keep the reader's attention focused on the idea, not the image or the language. If a gag seems particularly strong, I draw it in a deliberately offhand, crude fashion to underline that strength. The contrast can be powerful. I have a friend who is very beautiful. But her beauty is given an exceptional power by the fact that she is in a wheelchair. Bob Dylan chose to sing the very powerful lyrics of "Don't Think Twice" or "Blowin' in the Wind" in a tired, scratchy voice backed by rudimentary guitar. I can draw beautifully if that's what's called for. But it almost never is. A clown's job is to be grotesque; so he wears baggy pants and outsize shoes.

With drawing I can convey the nobility of the human animal caught in an oppressive world. My characters look round-shouldered, often abused. There is shock and disillusionment in their eyes. They could be Kurtz, in Conrad's *Heart of Darkness,* whispering, "The horror. The horror."

Comedy is the main weapon we have against "The Horror." With it we can strike a blow at death itself. Or, at least, poke a hole in the pretentious notion that there is something dignified about it.

At the suggestion of one of my English professors, I once drew a version of Dante's "Inferno" as a strip. He used to have me explain my gags in class because he loved to listen to the explanations. But it felt odd to be explaining, say, an anorexia gag to a roomful of affluent, self-absorbed debutantes with glazed eyes. I felt very much like a comedian who was dying onstage. I wanted to whip out a .38 and blow the class away because their nonreaction told me clearly: "Callahan, you missed your calling, you should have been an aluminum-siding salesman."

I'm gifted with a natural "gag sense," which allows me to invent twists that somehow reflect back on the original cliché. I love the old gag about the man in the electric chair. The warden hands him a roast and says, "Would you mind holding this? My wife's oven is on the blink." Of course I immediately felt compelled to top it.

I was born driven. Even when I was four years old, I was compulsive about being creative. I've never stopped. I can come up with a joke, a rhyme in the middle of *anything*. I draw right from the guts. It's a joy, but it's also painful at times, like giving birth. It's a calling. It's a burden. And it's a curse.

"He's our auxiliary power source."

Someone wrote a letter to an editor saying, "Building humor on the handicaps of a victim of some accident is . . . base and without merit. This type of laughter ridicules outcomes that were not freely chosen and conditions that cannot be reversed by the victim." I reserve the right to draw gags about any group or individual, especially about self-righteous types who presume to defend the disabled. What is interesting is the way the writer, in trying to make a simple distinction, ends up ruling out whole areas—in fact, the primary areas—of comedy: combat humor, gallows humor, ghetto humor, humor based on poverty, or on anything else that is not "freely chosen."

My mind resembles a Venus flytrap, always poised and ready. If a gag even comes close, I snap shut on it, and I exclude nothing. . . . Frankly, I don't care if gags like that get me run out of town by a mob with pitchforks and torches, or if they pin a medal on me.

I am sometimes labeled as part of a Northwest school or movement in cartooning, comprising Lynda Barry, Gary Larson, Matt Groening, Jim Blashfield, and Bill Plympton, among others. Sometimes the list is extended to include writers, notably Todd Grimson and Katherine Dunn, whose wit is also more than a little macabre. Something about these gray, misty mornings, maybe, infuses our work with a grim but hilarious tone. It has also been suggested that living here, far from the trendoids of New York or L.A., we are like a bunch of exiles, looking in at America from the outside.

I don't know about all that. I view my career as having passed through three periods. First came my "black" period. Then as I developed, I entered a "black" period. Now my horizons have widened, and I feel myself to have passed through to a third, or "black," period. God knows what comes next.

A LEAD BALLOON

In the course of being a "big-time cartoonist," I've had many fulfilling accomplishments. I've been lucky enough to have most of my work accepted and published. However, I have experienced many heartbreaking failures and an incredible amount of rejection too. And so it is with a certain embarrassment and hesitation that I now share various ill-conceived attempts at the perfect cartoon strip.

My desire has always been to break new ground and to push the envelope. What could be more edgy than a cartoon strip whose main character is deceased? "Mrs. Venable" was that—an elderly woman who is slumped over dead from a heart attack. My intent was to present a strip in which absolutely no action took place, and my plan was to publish the exact same cartoon of this dead woman, week after week.

"Mrs. Venable" was rejected by every editor to whom it was submitted. It was considered to be simply too much. Most of the newspapers felt the concept was too morbid, too depressing.

The strip, however, was accepted with wild enthusiasm by Suzanne, a girl I was dating at the time.

"Theatre of the Stricken" was my attempt at dazzling the cartoon world. On its back rode all the hopes and dreams of a frustrated and misunderstood cartoonist. Surely the concept of mentally and physically challenged sideshow performers could be considered viable and compelling. This was not the case, alas, and "Theatre of the Stricken" never found its way into newsprint.

"Genetic Gene" was also misunderstood and cruelly rejected out of hand by shallow and evil editors who deemed it offensive and unsavory. Little did they know what ecstatic pleasure the strip would bring to several close friends who read it in my living room one night, ten years later.

"No Witnesses" was a strip about a blind, disembodied head on a crash cart, begging at a street corner. As with "Mrs. Venable," the concept escaped more than one fine editor. It was considered too dark and was termed, by Bill Lee, cartoon editor of *Omni* magazine, a "grotesque farce."

48

DICKS

This is a series of jokes that never penetrated the fickle folds of the magazine markets.

HUMAN SEXUALITY 202
PROF. DANELLE

"...working upward from the scrotum, we have the shaft, the glans...?"

"Richard, you've slipped away from me again."

"Honey, the vacuum cleaner's plugged up again!"

"But you seemed so excited in the bar when I
I told you I had a big dick!"

"But MRs. Wilson, I thought you asked me if I Had a sack!"

"I hate these old movies! The lips are always out of sync with the sound!"

" See how the man keeps the monkey chained to his organ ? "

" Give me everything you've got ! "

SNAP... CRACKLE... POP?

When Leonard Buzzcock and I turned seventeen, we decided we needed to get prostitutes. So we drove two hundred miles to Seattle, where we could be more anonymous, and besides, there was only one hooker in our small town. Her name was "Horny Helen," and all the guys used to get her drunk and take her into the hobo jungles. The thought of that ancient, crab-infested orifice made our dicks vibrate with fear and horror, and so off to Seattle we sped in Leonard's father's 1966 Thunderbird.

We arrived at dusk on a sultry summer evening with a lust that seemed unbearable. I was nauseated with excitement! To think of a big-city whore, maybe in her thirties, vastly experienced in the ways of wickedness, taking me on a magic carpet ride into carnal ecstasy, perhaps even heightening my experience with an unexpected comment like "Well, hello, monster-meat." At the least, she might perceive me as a "sinewy country stud," even though I was a skinny, pale-skinned geek with thick glasses.

My chest was heaving as we drove down the famous Yester Street. The hookers were virtually lined up along the curb.

"Let's get black hookers!" screamed Leonard.

"Okay," I said, "how 'bout those two right over there!!" Halfway down the block stood two shapely black girls, dressed in miniskirts and go-go boots. I could see they were pretty, or at least very sexy in heavy makeup and revealing blouses.

"Say something to 'em!" barked Leonard, as he slowed down at the curb.

"I . . . I . . . I . . ."

"You boys wants a date?" purred the one wearing a cowboy hat.

"Ah . . . yeah . . . we're from The Dalles."

"Shut up, you idiot!!" muttered Leonard beneath his breath. "Do you want them to know we're gomers?!"

"Hop in!" he said.

As I lurched forward to let them climb in the backseat, I knocked my glasses off and they clanked into the gutter.

"Shit!" groaned Leonard.

"No problem, heh heh!" I chirped. But I grimaced inwardly at my clumsiness as I slapped them back on my face. How stupid of me to draw attention to the very object that symbolized my lack of virility.

"How much?" asked Leonard, after the girls had settled in the backseat and we were pulling away into traffic.

"Thirty for a screw and twenty for a blow job."

"We've only got forty, I guess we'll just take the blow jobs," answered Leonard, sounding surprisingly authoritative and citified.

The money then was passed back to them, and the hookers stuffed it into their purses.

"Okay," said the main whore, "we gots to go to the alley behind the Oriental Hotel. Just keep goin' straight and I's tells you where to turn."

I was dizzy with anxiety and anticipation. The smell of perfume was overwhelming. I swung my arm over the back of my seat and turned my head to view our newly purchased ladies of the night.

"You both look lovely this evening," I said.

"Thanks," said the main whore, staring straight ahead.

The other girl was constantly checking out the back window, presumably for vice cops. She was the prettier of the two and the younger, probably under thirty. She had her hair pulled up, and her neck was long and graceful. Her large breasts were nearly bursting out of her exposed lacy bra. She had on a red leather miniskirt, which revealed her garter attachments. "Wow, a real woman!" I thought, wincing with pleasure at the thought of the little piece of heaven she would soon provide me.

The main whore had smaller breasts, but she had a savage sexiness to her face. She had a velvet strap tightly wrapped around her neck and a gold medallion pinned on the side of her cowboy hat. What struck me most was the size of both girls. Not only were they large boned and buxom, but they were both unusually tall. They were huge. They must have been six feet tall. Of course this only added to the intensity of my anticipation. It was going to happen at last! We were going to get laid by some big-city hookers! I looked over at Leonard, and he gave me a thumbs up and a wink. Our dicks were vibrating with rural virility and impending triumph.

"Turn in here," said the main whore. "Drive around to the back of the hotel. Now pull in under one of those eaves and shut ya motor and lights off."

"She's *so* forceful!" I thought. I shivered, picturing her gasping face gorging my manly member. We were parked in a dimly lit alley with nothing but abandoned cars everywhere. It seemed safe and totally quiet.

"Okay," said the main whore, "climb back here."

The younger whore moved to the front seat next to Leonard. I took my place in the back next to the main whore. It had gotten a bit chilly, and I asked if I could roll up the window.

"Go ahead," said the main whore, "it's your car!"

She didn't seem amorous at all. "She'll become more sensuous as the evening wears on," I reassured myself.

"Oh shit! I ain't got no rubbers in here!" She was rifling through her handbag angrily. She was very intimidating in her annoyance.

"You got any, Ramona?"

"Shit no, honey. I ain't got a one!"

"Shee-it!!" cried the main whore, "now what's we gonna do?"

"Do you really need rubbers just for blow jobs?" asked Leonard.

"I ain't touchin' nobody's bare-ass dick, honey! And that's for sho!" she retorted. She seemed huge beside me. I felt silly with my pants around my ankles and my knobby knees trembling next to this giant whore.

In the rearview mirror, I could see Leonard's eyes looking back at me. I knew he was thinking the same panicky thoughts I was thinking.

"What's this?" said the main whore, reaching to the floor and retrieving a large piece of cellophane in her hand.

"That's a wrapper from a pie we bought at the convenience store," I answered.

"Well, it'll have to do," growled the main whore. "It's all we got." She ripped the piece of cellophane in two and handed half of it to the other hooker.

"Let's go," said the main hooker and she slid over close to me. I was only halfway hard as she forced the plastic wrapper around my trembling penis. She then lowered her giant head down to my lap and began bobbing and stroking so forcefully that the car began to rock. Bang! Bang! Bang! Bang . . . Bang . . . Bang! The springs in the seat were creaking, Bang . . . Bang . . . Bang! I could feel my own head bobbing to and fro as she continued her assault on my genitals. "How long can I take this bludgeoning?!" I thought.

"Are you coming yet?" the annoyed but muffled voice called out.

"No," I said, but my response could barely be heard above the deafening crackle of crinkling cellophane. Crackle! Crackle! CRACKLE!!! I could hear the crackle of cellophane from the front seat where poor Leonard was receiving his own abuse. Crackle! Crackle! CRACKLE!!!

"You comin' yet?" barked the main whore.

"No."

The crackling was so utterly distracting, I could concentrate on nothing else. It sounded like a nuclear reactor.

Just when I thought things couldn't get any worse, my eyes met Leonard's in the rearview mirror. Now I was staring into the eyes of another heterosexual male as my genitals were being stimulated. Leonard reached up and turned the mirror upward. Crackle! Crackle! CRACKLE!!! It was the only sound in the universe. I feared the vice cops would hear it!

"You better come soon, boy!" she warned, and the bobbing and jerking became so violent I feared I'd soon need Dramamine!

"This is a nightmare," I thought as I felt myself growing smaller and smaller.

"What's a matter with you, boy? You got sumpin' wrong with you? I ain't gonna go at this forever. I's done. Ramona, you all done? Let's get outa here—I can't do nuthin' with this limp-dick squirt!"

The whores straightened themselves up, grabbed their handbags, and climbed back out into the night.

I just sat there for the longest time, all alone in that cold backseat with my pants around my ankles. I didn't feel like a sinewy country stud. I felt like a little white worm. Like a little white worm with thick glasses. Like the littlest, whitest worm, with the thickest glasses in the world, and my dick looked like a tiny pink mushroom, a moist and delicate mushroom tenderly placed amid the jagged roughness of a dark and hostile forest. I thought of all the dicks that preceded mine. Dicks that had made it through the crackling. Dicks that had succeeded.

"Ready to go, Johnny?" came Leonard's voice from the front seat.

"Yeah."

We pulled away from the darkness of the Oriental and hit the freeway. On the long drive home our dicks vibrated with shame and loathing.

When we finally pulled up to my parents' house, Leonard got out and opened the back car door for me.

"What'll I do now?" I asked.

"Pull up your pants and go in the house," said Leonard.

I crawled into bed, stared into the dark. Perhaps the words of the K-Man were true:

"Oh, what a tangled web we weave when first we take a shot at the 'Beave.'"

Peter,
Paul,
and
Mary —
in the
Year 2000.

CALLAHAN

FAN AND OTHER MAIL

The only thing worse than being harassed is not being harassed. I've enjoyed the keen interest shown by many of my readers over the years in their letters to the editor. Truthfully, I have not gone out of my way to disturb people. I've only tried to please myself and my friends. It's just that topics that excite my friends and me are, I guess, disturbing!

I've never been the kind of cartoonist who is interested in typical cartoon themes like pets, dieting, the boss at work, etc. Life to me is major league, and I'm drawn to the aspects of it that typify the struggle: death, disease, insanity, feminism, tragedy, disability, etc.

Though my work also includes themes of sweetness and frivolity, I'm afraid I've been cruelly and unjustly typecast as sick and twisted. Let it be known that I have never once answered any of the "lively" letters aimed at me. Except once, when I could no longer abide the criticism that "Mr. Callahan could not possibly understand the struggle of someone with a spinal injury."

Anyway, here are just a few of my favorite of the many slings and arrows that have come my way over the years. Also, a few with differing points of view.

OUT OF TOON?

Dear Editor:

I'm baffled by the weekly appearance of Callahan cartoons (Palm Latitudes). Any one of the daily single-panel comics in the Times' View section would be more worthy of inclusion than the poorly drawn and unfunny Callahan.

Barbara B.
Claremont, California

Los Angeles Times
May 23, 1993

February 13, 1993

Levin Represents
Hoboken, New Jersey

Dear Sirs,

I am currently a guest at a hotel in Boston, where there is a card store in the lobby. I noticed a highly distasteful and absolutely DISGRACEFUL postcard on the shelf. It was a John Callahan card that showed a group of cowboys in the dirt, with an empty wheelchair. The caption read "Don't Worry, He Won't Get Far on Foot."

My brother sits in a wheelchair, a quadriplegic, as a result of a diving accident at 19. Until Mr. Callahan can understand the emotions behind such a life of struggle, I feel he should not feel so freely about poking fun at the disabled. I find your marketing of his insensitivity positively DISGUSTING!

Sincerely,

Allison F.

MEDIA ACCESS OFFICE INC.
DISABILITY RESOURCE TO THE ENTERTAINMENT INDUSTRY

September 19, 1991

John Callahan
Portland, Oregon

Dear John,

Congratulations! On behalf of the Board of Directors of the Media Access Office, it is a pleasure to notify you that you have been selected to receive the Outstanding Contribution by an Individual award for the 13th Annual Media Access Awards.

The history of these awards spans thirteen years, originally beginning as a project of the California Governor's Committee for Employment of Disabled Persons. The Media Access Office is a disability resource to the Entertainment Industry, providing casting and technical assistance, as well as recognition. The awards recognize the efforts of the mass media to integrate images that counteract negative stereotypes of persons with disabilities. . . .

Sincerely,

Jenny Gerard
Executive Director

It was too good to be true.

August 19, 1994

To: John Callahan, *Don't Worry, He Won't Get Far on Foot*

From: David N., Spinal Cord Injured Nov. 5, 1992

Re: Letter of Appreciation

Dear Mr. Callahan:

I'm about halfway through your autobiography—and loving it! Your cartoons
are fantastic. I was hospitalized at Harbor General for 2½ weeks. Then I was
transferred to Cedars-Sinai in L.A. for 4 months. Wow, I can really relate to your
writing.

If you have a fan club, please let me know about it. Also, let me know if you've
published any other books.

Thank you for your time and keep up the great work.

Yours truly,

David N.
West Hollywood, California

"Run for your life! It's the Sally Struthers car alarm!!!"

SHARP & ASSOCIATES _____

public relations

January 19, 1993

Bret Israel, Editor
Los Angeles Times Magazine

Bret Israel,

I represent Sally Struthers and feel compelled to take exception to the humorless Callahan cartoon which ran on your Palm Latitudes page on Sunday January 17. It is so unfortunate that your magazine, and indeed the Los Angeles Times itself, finds it amusing that Sally Struthers has worked so diligently for so many years to try to end the starvation and suffering of children in this world.

Sally's tireless work for 17 years has been an attempt to end world hunger . . . Somalia just being the tip of the iceberg. Your publication insinuates that in the ads she makes for CCF she cries ("sobs") while she talks about the children. I defy you to find a single advertisement she has made in those 17 years in which she cries . . . yes, she speaks from the heart, but, no she doesn't cry! . . .

For the children,

Pamela Sharp

LEVINE & MILLER

January 19, 1993

Mr. David Laventhol, Publisher
Los Angeles Times Magazine
Los Angeles, California

Dear Mr. Laventhol:

While I am Sally Struthers' attorney, I am also her friend. In both capacities I was outraged by the distasteful and hurtful cartoon which Mr. Callahan and the staff of the Los Angeles Times Magazine mistook for humor in the January 17, 1993 edition of the L.A. Times Magazine page 13. My wife and I have been among the supporters of the Christian Children's Fund for many years and we have been personal friends with Sally and watched her herculean efforts to try to mend a small part of the world's woes and ameliorate the punishment inflicted upon the children who are the innocent and unknowing victims of hunger, poverty and oppression.

It seems Mr. Callahan feels that Sally's efforts deserve a below the belt blow which he delivered under the guise of freedom of the press and in abuse of the First Amendment. He obviously feels he is invulnerable in his tainted ivory tower along with the other people whom you hire to "edit" the Magazine safe from the slings of arrows of outraged subjects and their friends. . . .

I look forward to your response.

Very truly yours,

Gunther H. Schiff

GUNTHER H. SCHIFF

February 2, 1995

John Callahan
c/o Noble Works
Hoboken, New Jersey

Re: *Sally Struthers*

Dear Mr. Callahan:

. . . You should be ashamed of yourself!

The fact that you are, as I am informed, an angry quadriplegic does not sanction in any way your misogynistic attack on Ms. Struthers.

My client would deeply appreciate it if you would eliminate her name from any use in the sale of your perverted humor, for which you have become famous, or perhaps infamous.

Very truly yours,

Gunther H. Schiff

MORE CALLAHANS, PLEASE

Dear Editor:

Enough! Every week readers of the Letters page endure the whining and moaning of those who object to the Callahan cartoons.

If they had their way, these narrow-minded, self-appointed humor critics would have us laughing only at what they approved as suitably funny.

I propose that the editor eliminate these letters of hand wringing and angst and, in their place, put another Callahan cartoon!

Keep up the great work, Callahan. We need someone like you to keep us from getting too full of ourselves.

Tom S.
Palatine

Chicago Tribune Magazine
December 25, 1994

Jack! you're too drunk - you need a "designated stumbler"!
JOE'S BAR
CALLAHAN

Dear Editor:

   Please cancel the Callahan cartoons. They seem to be getting more and more offensive, and they're always aimed at women!

   That women complained about sexual harassment only if they think the guy isn't cute? Who is this Neanderthal jerk?

   And what about the way he draws the women in the office? What office is this where the women wear such low-cut, tight dresses? His cartoons are similar to ethnic jokes in that his slurs in the guise of humor help keep alive damaging stereotypes.

   Dump this loser—he's not funny.

Lucy B.
Chicago

Chicago Tribune Magazine
January 29, 1995

CALLAHAN

Dear Editor:

The Callahan cartoon of Jan. 9 made me very upset. In a year the United Nations has dedicated to the family, this type of journalism is very pessimistic and creates a negative psychological atmosphere in any woman that wants to make her home a nice one for her family. There is nothing wrong with cleaning, and it does not make you stupid. A clean and pleasant house brings people together and makes them rest better.

The roots of crime are in the lack of a real home for young delinquents and with nasty cartoons you are not helping that cause.

Rosa Mary A.
Delray Beach

Tropic, the Sunday magazine of *The Miami Herald*
February 13, 1994

CARTOONIST CALLAHAN AT THE CENTER OF CONTROVERSY, AGAIN

[The dog/donkey cartoon] has provoked a profound rage among readers I never would have predicted. . . . Phone calls and letters have attacked the cartoon as sexist and not worthy of Downtown News. Readers were appalled, insulted . . . they did not think the cartoon was funny.

I thought the cartoon was profane, but not sexist. I allowed the editorial staff to print it because I thought it was fall-down funny, easily amusing enough and important enough in its satire to justify the profanity that accompanied it. . . .

To me it was what Callahan does best. He satirized a tired old sexist remark with a play on words. Rather than sexist, I saw it as liberating, a cartoon that ridiculed people who talk like that.

I didn't stand totally alone this time, but close. Some staff members cringed; some loved it. Even Callahan's publicist was amazed we'd printed it. "Everyone thinks it's funny," she said, "but no one else has had the courage to print it."

John Callahan, the quadriplegic cartoonist whose stuff we obtain from his syndicate, is an iconoclast of the first order. He calls many politically correct themes and narrow presumptions into question, particularly those relating to the handicapped. But humor is always the dominant factor of his work, and his incisive eye extends well beyond the issues of the handicapped.

He has offended people before, and he will no doubt do so again. This time he called from his apartment in Portland to comment on the dog/donkey cartoon. He confirmed he intended it as a satire. He was as amazed at the outcry as I was. . . .

Sue Laris-Eastin
Editor and Publisher

Los Angeles Downtown News
July 15, 1992

MORE CALLAHAN FALLOUT

Dear Editor:

I was wondering how long it would take for your newspaper to degenerate into a journalistic rag. Well, that extremely distasteful cartoon by Callahan in your July 6 edition did the trick! His portrayal of the dog and jackass and the two hard-hat characters along with the quote "Look at the ass on that bitch" certainly was an offensive, veiled expression often used to describe women.

Decent and sensitive women—including Callahan's mother, sister, daughter, wife—deplore this kind of degradation. If the cartoon's meaning was supposed to be a covert, satirical joke, it was not, because the intent bled through.

Alice W.

Los Angeles Downtown News
July 15, 1992

RICHARD PRYOR

August 22, 1995

Dear Ms. Levin:

Rumor is correct! I am a Callahan fan! Thank you so much for the great Callahan cards. My favorite one, naturally, is "Look at the ass on that bitch!"

Your kindness and consideration is sincerely appreciated.

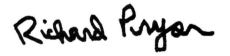

FEMINIST DATE

I asked a woman out the other night. I saw her at a supermarket and she made it easy for me. When I came around the corner, she smiled lovingly at me. I went right up to her and started talking. We hit it off quickly and talked for half an hour, and I asked her to coffee on Saturday.

All week long I thought of her, fanaticizing in a somewhat restrained fashion. After twenty-five years of dating on and off, I've learned not to set myself up for what seems to end up in disappointment. But it's always difficult to hold back. I cannot help but build up the girl in my imagination as the dream woman who will understand me like no other could. She will recognize the great suffering and depth of character with one glance into my eyes. She will be shaken by the force of my charisma, tempered by a quiet humility and graceful serenity. My smoldering sensuality will weaken her knees as she ultimately realizes I am the one who will finally set her free from the chains of her mind-bending unfulfillment. Yes, she will call her girlfriend and will be able only to gasp spasmodically, unable to communicate the nature of her great fortune.

Saturday finally came around and I headed down to the coffee shop with my now elaborate fantasies. I'm early. I'll just order a coffee and lounge charismatically near the back of the shop, waiting for her. "Ah, there she is!" My heart pounds with excitement as I notice her advancing toward me. She is smiling and waving as she weaves her way through the crowd. "Wait a minute," I think as a wave of disappointment passes through me. "She's not wearing any makeup! She had makeup on when I met her!" My disappointment deepens as I realize she had pulled her hair back and tied a sloppy knot behind her head.

"Hi." She smiles as she sits down heavily across from me. "I decided to jog here since I won't be able to later today."

"That's great," I retort. "You jog a lot then?"

"Oh yeah," she gasps, still out of breath.

I order her a cup of coffee.

"Decaf, if you please," she says. "I'm sorry I'm late but I had to stop off and pick up some Tampax at the Swift-Mart!"

"Oh yes." I smile weakly at the little sack in her hand.

"I'm gonna have to split early here 'cause I'm manning the volunteer hot line at this feminist crisis center in the morning. . . . So you're the cartoonist, huh? What's it like, being a cartoonist? Is it fun being recognized by people?"

"Oh, it's kinda fun, I guess." Was she wearing wire-rimmed glasses when I first met her?

"My contacts were bugging me so I wore my trusty glasses. I'll be right back. I had a twelve-grain croissant for breakfast and, well, you never know. . . ." I watched her making her way toward the rest room and I felt that old familiar sense of doom. Panic and rage descended over me.

She returned, chatting enthusiastically, stirring her mocha. "Maybe you'd like to join in the 'Take back the night' parade I'm organizing. It's primarily a women's event, but we're allowing a few men to follow behind us, discussing the different ways they've oppressed women throughout the centuries. . . ." I was drifting further into a state of dissociation. I couldn't even feel the pain anymore. Why me? Why me? Why . . .

Dear Editor:

I know John Callahan is even now penning better rebuttals to his detractors, and so I'm not doing this on his behalf.

I want you to leave Callahan's cartoon right where it is and stop giving so much letter space to the babies whining about him not goose-stepping to the beat of the politically correct or—and I loved this—intimating that your magazine is "liberal" (read "pinko").

Hey, my feminist credentials are in order. It's just not true that we don't have a sense of humor. I'd feel left out if he didn't offend me once in a while. Meanwhile, I carry around his cartoon of the psychiatrist telling the satyr on his office couch to "Stop blaming your parents." I carry this cartoon like we carried around holy cards in our missals when it was only the kids like John Callahan who kept me from going berserk during my infinitely long tenure in Catholic schools.

I'm so politically incorrect, by the way, that I'm still in love with Jimmy Carter, Ralph Nader, Henry Miller and, maybe, I need to add for the sake of absolute honesty, still a bit in love with Woody Allen.

Maryellen G.
Brookfield

Chicago Tribune Magazine
March 23, 1994

Dear Editor:

   Callahan may have some sexist attitudes, but does this mean his comic should be cancelled from the Magazine, as suggested in earlier letters?

   I'm sick of this "Let's hang the alternative artist thing because they don't confirm and reaffirm our every belief."

   Cartoonists can learn a lot from readers' constructive criticism, but suggestions to "can" Callahan are a pretty harsh sentence.

   At least Callahan is honest, which is more than I can say for a lot of the boring, watered-down stuff out in the world today. If you want to do something about sexism, go picket the strip clubs.

Heather M.
Chicago

Chicago Tribune Magazine
March 23, 1994

6:00

⑦ ⑧ ⑤ ⑩ **60 Minutes** — Shark cartilage, a treatment for cancer; efforts of St. Petersburg, Fla., to get a major league baseball team; cartoonist John Callahan

A Nocturnal Omission *

The *Miami Herald*'s
brain trust comes to grips
with a sticky wicket

By Jim DeFede

This past Wednesday, as the devastating Oklahoma City bomb blast sent the nation's news media into a tizzy, the *Miami Herald*'s management was frantically conferring about another calamity far closer to home. Hands were wrung, teeth were gnashed. Fingers were pointed. It was an event that Tom Shroder, executive editor of the *Herald*'s *Tropic* magazine, describes as "the greatest nightmare of my entire journalism career."

It was the *Callahan* affair.

As they do every Wednesday morning, 530,000 copies of the magazine had rolled off the presses to join other sections of the Sunday *Herald* that are produced in advance. And as usual a stack had made its way from the print shop to *Tropic*'s editorial department. No sooner had the office manager turned to the second page of the issue, however, than it became apparent that something was terribly amiss. Shroder was quickly notified. Staring down at the page, the editor felt his cheeks flush. Before the magazine had gone to press, Shroder had culled a batch of submissions from cartoonist John Callahan. But page

two of *Tropic* didn't contain the *Callahan* Shroder had selected; it bore a different work by the artist, a cartoon Shroder had specifically *rejected* because he found it offensive.

"It was like a rattlesnake jumped off the page and bit me in the face," recalls the editor.

Drawn in Callahan's trademark square style, the panel depicts a thirteen-year-old Martin Luther King, Jr., standing next to his bed, in the middle of which is a large puddle. "I had a dream," the boy says, as his mother looks on disapprovingly.

"It was so tasteless and so offensive, the most offensive cartoon he has ever sent us," says Shroder, adding that no one has

yet been able to trace the source of the goof.

The anxious editor considered his options. By this time the press run had been completed; copies of the magazine already were being inserted into the *Herald*'s travel section. Some had been loaded onto trucks and delivered to distribution sites around Dade, where they awaited the remainder of the Sunday edition.

The only solution Shroder could think of was a drastic one. He contacted Doug Clifton, the *Herald*'s executive editor, and suggested that the entire issue of *Tropic* be printed over again—all 530,000 copies. Managing editor Saundra Keyes was brought in on the discussion, and after an emergency summit with publisher David Lawrence, Jr., it was agreed that the magazine would be run off again with a different cartoon. Crews were dispatched country-wide to extract each and every copy of the magazine, one at a time, by hand. "[*Tropic* editor] Bill Rose and I physically ripped the page out of every copy we could find in the office," Shroder says.

The next day *Tropic* was reprinted with a cartoon by Tom White substituted for *Callahan.* To solve the insertion problem, the magazine was placed inside the *Herald*'s Sunday classifieds. Total cost, including the price of collecting the banned copies: $45,000.

"'I Have a Dream' is the single most identifiable statement about the yearnings of an entire oppressed people, and here it was tossed off in a very crude masturbation joke," explains Tom Shroder. "It was not making a legitimate observation about anything. And the art itself was verging on pornographic—the actual portrayal of bodily fluids."

Shroder is the man who introduced Miami to the humor of John Callahan, a cartoonist whose work appears in a handful of newspapers nationwide. In an August 1989 column that welcomed *Callahan* to *Tropic,* Shroder compared the artist with Garry Trudeau, creator of *Doonesbury,* and Berke Breathed, of *Bloom County* fame. "Enter, extreme stage left John Callahan, guerrilla cartoonist," the editor wrote. Elucidating the cartoonist's perverse appeal, Shroder offered a close reading of one of Callahan's more grotesque efforts: "The Low Ceiling Fan Café"is a cartoon pic-

turing a stream of people stumbling out the door of an eatery headless and spurting blood: Callahan, full strength. Indigestible? That's what they said about Trudeau. Callahan is not funny in spite of his darker stuff. He is funny because of it." Shroder also described Callahan's humor as "liberating."

That same 1989 issue of *Tropic* included a lengthy profile of John Callahan, chronicling the artist's life and discussing his quadriplegia, the result of a car accident. "I'm happiest when I'm offensive," reads one Callahan quote from the piece. "I have a desire to tear people in half. I want to move people out of the suburbs of their mind. I want them to suffer, to feel something real. I have a lot of anger. I want to hurt people. At least a little." (John Callahan did not return messages seeking his comment about the current controversy.)

Evidently Miami's only daily didn't want its readers pulled quite *that* far out of the suburbs of their minds.

Ken Conner, the Sunday editor for the *San Francisco Chronicle,* which also features Callahan's work, says his paper didn't run this particular submission, either. "Honestly, I laughed when I saw that cartoon," Conner admits. "But a lot of that was just laughing at what Callahan gets away with." While *Herald* editors assert that their primary concern was the cartoon's racial insensitivity, Conner says he was more worried about its explicit nature. "I'm not afraid of making fun of Martin Luther King—he is as fair a target as anyone," says the *Chronicle* editor.

"And [Shroder] is wrong, it really isn't a masturbation joke, it was a nocturnal-emission joke. That's where we drew the line: We don't like jokes that use bodily functions. In this cartoon, the amount of semen on the bed, well, it was just too graphic for us."

Herald publisher David Lawrence goes a step further. "This cartoon fits my definition of what is trash." Lawrence says. "I wouldn't want to work for a newspaper that printed that."

Echoes Doug Clifton, the paper's executive editor. "It was awful. It could not run in a reputable newspaper that had any sensitivity to the people it serves."

Ten years ago Mark Zusman was one of the first editors in the U.S. to feature *Callahan,* in the *Willamette Week,* an alternative weekly in the artist's hometown of Portland, Oregon. "Callahan is a pretty black-humor guy. His humor is completely and utterly opaque," says Zusman, who recently ran the controversial cartoon. "That's what is so precious about the guy. Occasionally I run cartoons of his that make me wince. But that's part of the cost of having someone who steps right up to the line: Every now and then he might step over it. We afford him that opportunity. With Callahan, you buy the package and you take the good with the bad."

In the future, Miamians may not have to worry about either extreme. According to Doug Clifton, *Callahan*'s long-term fate is under review. "I've never been a fan of it," Clifton says. "It is an element of *Tropic* I've never been fond of, and this just heightens that."

Dear Editor:

Hey! Where are the John Callahan gags that used to grace the space beneath *Up Front*? His cartoons are funny, biting and necessary, in these days of "political correctness." Is The Miami Herald running scared? Closing its eyes to one of the most important things the print media can do for our TV/computer/techno pop-eyed age? Make people want to think! Tell it like it is; sing the truth in your pages. (As close to the truth as you can reach.) That's why you need the work of a man like Callahan. He is not afraid to take on truth; his cartoons are meant to help us laugh at it (at times when truth hurts). I hate to say this but are we living in a time when the ignorance of mob thinking is stifling the freedom of the press? Say it isn't so, please bring back Callahan's gags.

Don and Norma M.
Miami

Tropic, the Sunday magazine of
The Miami Herald
March 13, 1995

Up Front from the Editor: Standing Room Only*

It has nearly been a year now since we published a very heartfelt, articulate letter from a woman outraged by a Callahan cartoon depicting a clinic filled with quadriplegics staring forlornly across the street at a church vibrating with the hymn *You'll Never Walk Alone*. . . .

Some time later, we received another letter that I kept, but never published: "I respond as an expert on the subject," Jack Schaefer wrote. "I've been a quad for 26 years. Of course, the newly injured are devastated by their injury, but once they accept the fact, they usually return to normality (to the extent they can). This includes their sense of humor. The letter writer sounds as if she thinks the spinal cord injured want pity. We don't. I believe she means well, but I for one don't need someone not in my shoes speaking for me. I personally love Callahan."

Today [here] are two new Callahans likely to spark the same debate. In the nearly four years since Callahan's work has been a weekly Tropic feature, we've noticed something interesting: When we get complaints about his handling of the subject of disability, they are almost always from people without disabilities themselves. And whenever we hear from the physically disabled, individually and through organizations promoting their interests, what we hear is loud and enthusiastic applause.

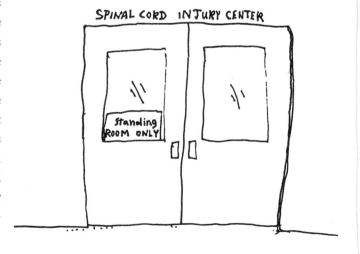

*Reprinted from *Tropic,* the Sunday magazine of *The Miami Herald,* February 28, 1993, by permission of the publisher.

Perhaps that isn't too surprising, since Callahan is a quad himself. Callahan—who is scheduled to be the subject of a *60 Minutes* profile tonight on CBS (unless preempted)—reports that he has had the same experience: "For some reason, people with hooks for hands particularly love my cartoons," he says. "I've never had a handicapped person wheel up to me and say, 'How can you do those cartoons?' I don't think able-bodied people who are out there protecting all us quadriplegics have a leg to stand on."

The man is incorrigible. But the truth is, you shouldn't have to know that Callahan himself is disabled to realize that his cartoons are not "poking fun at the handicapped." The reason why our disabled readers love Callahan is they don't misread him. Look below. Is it a joke at the expense of people in wheelchairs? Hardly. Here's a clinic specifically designed for the disabled—presumably run by able-bodied doctors who don't understand the needs of the people they serve. Standing Room Only. The joke's on those of us who *can* stand.

Tom Shroder

**"It's a Chevy with chrome wheels, tinted windows,
Hurst 4-shift, and a 283 with dual quads."**

"DON'T YOU LOVE IT WHEN THEY'RE STILL WARM FROM THE DRYER?"

Make us smile

Dear Editor:

What is with you people? After the mail you received complaining about the offensive KKK cartoon in Callahan, you now print one that spoofs sexual harassment.

Please, let's come into the 20th century and stop offending everyone on the planet. Can't your cartoon make us smile, not turn away in disgust? Thank you for understanding the feelings of women in the workplace.

Elizabeth J.
Chicago

Chicago Tribune Magazine
April 26, 1994

QUESTIONING CALLAHAN

I am writing with regard to the "Callahan" cartoon of April 10 depicting two members of the Ku Klux Klan enjoying the warmth of their costumes "fresh" from the dryer.

Though I personally am fortunate never to have fallen victim to persecution by any extremist group, you should be aware that for many of your readers, you have awakened memories of this group's deplorable activity.

Next time you feel the urge to publish such an item, I suggest you spend time reviewing it first with a slightly more diverse audience in order to avoid such a tasteless error.

Robert M.
Chicago

I found the Callahan cartoon anything but comic and to be in very poor taste. To say that I hope such themes as this do not repeat themselves is an understatement.

Teri T.
Park Forest

How could you even dignify the KKK by printing such a cartoon? To ignore is to marginalize. To satirize is to legitimize.

Susan L.
Wilmette

Chicago Tribune Magazine
April 19, 1994

TAKE A WALK ON THE WILDSIDE, INC.
THE CANADIAN CROSSDRESSERS CLUB
THE CANADIAN CrossDresser Magazine

Levin Represents
NobleWorks
Hoboken, New Jersey

Dear Sir or Madam:

We would like permission to reprint the [below] cartoon in our magazine, The Canadian CrossDresser, giving full credit to Callahan, Levin Represents and Nobleworks. We would of course, send a copy of the magazine in which the cartoon appears to you.

Thank you for your time.

Sincerely,

Veronica Brown
Editor

CALLAHAN

"YOU'RE A TRANSVESTITE, AREN'T YOU? I LIKE THAT IN A MAN!"

SLANTA CLAUS

ASO

CALLAHAN

94

MEDIA IMAGE COALITION

April 21, 1994

Deborah Levin
Santa Monica, California

Dear Ms. Levin:

The Media Image Coalition (MIC) was formed in 1990 under the auspices of the Los Angeles County Commission on Human Relations for the purpose of promoting balanced imagery and increased diversity in the portrayals of racial and ethnic minorities, women, gays and lesbians, seniors and people with disabilities in the media.

We are writing to express our deep concern about the Callahan cartoon [that] depicts a Santa Claus with "Asian" eyes and is captioned "Slanta Claus."

Not only is this message not particularly funny (racist implications aside), it is outrageously offensive and raises archaic and demeaning stereotypes about Asian-Americans.

Hate crime and Asian-bashing are on the rise in Los Angeles County. Your actions and those of your client, Mr. Callahan, in producing and disseminating this hateful message to more than 100 newspapers and magazines nationally only serves to exacerbate the problem. . . .

The MIC is available to you as a resource to assure greater sensitivity about the ever growing racial and cultural diversity of American society. We believe that our assistance would lead to an increased awareness about Asians and other ethnic and cultural groups. . . .

Sincerely,

Sumi Haru, Co-President
EEO Chair, AFTRA

Rodney Mitchell, Co-President
Executive Administrator
Affirmative Action, SAG

PACIFIC RIM INSTITUTE

of The American Jewish Committee

March 22, 1994

Deborah Levin
Deborah Levin Presents
Santa Monica, California

Dear Ms Levin:

The concerns of the Media Action Network for Asian Americans with insensitive and stereotypic images were brought to our attention. . . . Some of the cartoons by John Callahan were identified as cases in point.

The Pacific Rim Institute of the American Jewish Committee has joined with Asian American groups and some Asian Pacific nations in developing programs aimed at enhancing mutual understanding. . . .

We fully recognize and appreciate constitutional guarantees on freedom of expression. At the same time, we call on those involved in shaping opinion to recognize a special responsibility in dealing with groups that may be particularly vulnerable. As you know, the numbers of hate crimes directed against Asian Americans have grown significantly in recent years.

We are not seeking to characterize Mr. Callahan's cartoons in any special way, but, rather, to offer the observation that this is a particularly difficult time for those of Asian American background. Economic tensions between the U.S. and countries in Asia have a way of spilling over to the American cultural scene. . . .

It is our profound hope that Mr. Callahan will take these and other factors into consideration as he creates future cartoons.

Sincerely,

Neil C. Sandberg

"Let's wok the dog."

Editor:

I must express my complete indignation at the Callahan cartoon in your September 27 issue that featured an Asian male, Asian female and dog with the caption, "Let's wok the dog."

The cartoon is outrageous and racially insensitive despite its attempt at humor.

It is true that some Asian cultures eat domesticated animals for food. However, it should be known that, for decades, different Asian ethnic groups survived on animals such as dog to endure the ravages of famine and war. In light of this history, all Asians should not be the targets for such American abuse.

More disturbing is the fact that you found the cartoon clever enough to be acceptable for your paper. What you failed to recognize is that ignorance about many different ethnic communities runs rampant in our society.

Stereotypes, whether regarding Asians, Latinos or Blacks, define people's perceptions and help form their affinity or hatred for an ethnic group. If anything, the Downtown News should be committed to dismantling stereotypes instead of contributing to them.

Jimmy T.
Japanese American Citizens League

Editor:

I find the concept of mistreating and abusing animals, as displayed in Callahan's "Let's wok the dog" cartoon, to be very offensive.

It is a shame your publication is so insensitive.

Marilyn F.

Los Angeles Downtown News
October 18, 1993

To the editor:

I never before have bothered to respond to the "fashion-able" tastelessness of Callahan's cartoons, but my disgust meter shot off the scale when I saw the cartoon on page 9 of your Nov. 4, 1993 issue. The cartoon depicts a farm boy (Timmy?) and an older man looking over a rail fence. The boy asks the man, "Gee, Gramps, how long's it been since Lassie went over to visit the Wongs?"

Can it be that Callahan and the *Willamette Week* think there is a joke in the idea that a Chinese family would eat another family's pet? I figured I must have missed something. I showed the joke to several friends and co-workers. They each saw what I saw. They each recoiled with loathing.

Geoffrey W.

Willamette Week
November 24, 1993

参議院議員

八 代 英 太

Member of the House of Councillors
Diet of Japan
Tokyo, Japan

March 22, 1990

Mr. John Callahan
Portland, Oregon

Dear Mr. Callahan:

I am a wheelchair user and a member of parliament in Japan.

I watched a brief reporting on you on ABC news program broadcast here. Your effort is very encouraging. Consciousness raising through comics and cartoons is useful in changing attitude which forms one of the barriers for the equalization of opportunities.

I would be grateful if you could send me some information on your books and comics.

I look forward to hearing from you.

Yours very truly,

Eita Yashiro

RIPOFFS

They say the finest form of flattery is imitation. So take a look at this prick trying to rip me off!

NELSON, GUGGENHEIM, FELKER & LEVINE LLP
ATTORNEYS AT LAW
10880 WILSHIRE BOULEVARD, SUITE 2070
LOS ANGELES, CALIFORNIA 90024

Dear Mr. Belle:

This is a prima facie case of copyright infringement and trademark infringement which shall subject The City Paper to a claim for substantial damages by Mr. Callahan. You are hereby instructed to immediately cease and desist from running any Callahan cartoons, especially Callahan cartoons which have been misattributed and altered, and to call this office immediately to commence negotiations to pay damages for this offense. If you do not reach a reasonable settlement with this office, Mr. Callahan shall bring an action against you for copyright and trademark infringement, as well as other claims seeking punitive damages.

Very truly yours,

Peter Martin Nelson

MY DAY IN COURT

One afternoon the phone started ringing off the hook. "John!" everybody was saying. "Did you hear? You weren't watching the O.J. trial? Judge Ito just mentioned your name—right in the middle of the trial!"

"WHAT?!"

"It's true—he just mentioned you and your cartoons!"

The phone continued to ring with the news all day. Debbie Levin, my manager, called to say a friend of hers had videotaped the historic moment: Judge Ito, in the Trial of the Century, saying, "Why do I feel like I'm in the middle of a Callahan cartoon?"

"But how does Judge Ito know about *me?*" I asked her.

"Dummy," she laughed. "Your cartoons are in the *Los Angeles Times.*"

The Superior Court

Judge Lance A. Ito
Department 103
210 West Temple Street
Los Angeles, California 90012-3210
(213) 974-5726

25 August 1995

Deborah Levin
Santa Monica, California

Dear Ms. Levin:

Thank you for your thoughtfulness in sending me the Callahan cartoons and books. The "You've read the tabloids . . ." cartoon has been under the blotter on my bench since its original publication and has been both a warning and inspiration ever since. Please convey my admiration to Mr. Callahan.

Very truly yours,

Lance A. Ito

Court TV (LTV)
Transcript #131 Segment 1

August 14, 1995

Live Trial Coverage - CA v. Simpson - Day 131 - Part 1

FRED GRAHAM, Anchor: Welcome back. Things are slow getting underway this morning, and Judge Lance Ito's court. It's not all that unusual on a Monday morning, but delays have been occurring throughout this trial, and it's possible to foresee that maybe one more, at least, major delay is looming very soon down the line. And that is the matter of the so-called "Fuhrman tapes." If you follow the case at all you know that Detective Mark Fuhrman, a very controversial witness for the prosecution has been accused by the defense of being a racist who planted evidence out of racial animosity toward O.J. Simpson. In his testimony, Mark Fuhrman denied being a racist and denied, for at least 10 years back, ever having used the infamous "N" word. Well, it turns out that in his spare time, Mark Fuhrman had been consulting with and advising a screenwrite— screenwriter, a North Carolina woman, who was attempting to— to— to put to-

JOHNNIE COCHRAN, Simpson Atty.: We'll have some things to talk about, probably, this afternoon, but not until we get things going this afternoon.

Judge LANCE ITO: OK. I had anticipated this morning, 'cause I didn't bring the jury down.

JOHNNIE COCHRAN: Oh, the jury is— *[inaudible]* —OK. Thank you.

FRED GRAHAM: And while the attorneys are huddling here, I want to ask Tony Alexander what sort of delays do you think might occur because of these so-called "Fuhrman tapes?"

ANTHONY ALEXANDER, Crim. Defense Atty.: This is an area that, I think, is very critical to the proceedings in the case, and I think that Judge Ito, knowing the type of careful judge he is, will want to take as much time as necessary to review the tapes, listen to them, review the transcripts, give the prosecution and the defense an opportunity to prepare their thoughts and prepare motions. So I think it'll certainly be a fully litigated area because it is so crucial to the case at this time.

FRED GRAHAM: All right. And Johnnie Cochran seems to have cleared up whatever it was he wanted to huddle about, and we'll listen.

JOHNNIE COCHRAN: Your Honor, a couple of things

> **Judge LANCE ITO:** . . . I'm reminded of the Callahan cartoon that's often published regarding what the legal process appears to have become, and this is not a trial by news media, sources, leaks, tabloids or otherwise. The objection will be sustained on both grounds.

he had to leave.

Judge LANCE ITO: I recollect.

ROBERT BLASIER: We then called Agent Martz. I want to ask Dr. Rieders questions about Agent Martz's testimony. He has reviewed it. I told Ms. Clark that I have no objections if she just wants to start crossing him on that so we don't need to stop and recall him and that sort of thing. So if that's agreeable to Ms. Clark, that's fine with me.

MARCIA CLARK, Prosecutor: Yes. I've informed Mr. Blasier that'd be fine, that I'm not going to go through the rigmarole of having him leave and come back, or walk out the door and come back when he's recalled. That's fine. I'm not going to be able to completely cross-examine him on what he would be saying about Agent Martz, 'cause I really don't know until I hear the direct. So I'll have to reserve some of that for cross, but I'm going to make this as expeditious as possible, so—

Judge LANCE ITO: All right. Anything else we need to take up? Mr. Cochran?

I was back East this weekend. Your Honor, with regard to that, I would ask, with regard to the people who can listen to the tape, we've obviously got to expand it from the defense standpoint because Mr. Bailey is handling Detective Fuhrman, and we certainly anticipate that he's in the middle of cross-examination, so, it's kind of unfair that he can't— he has to know what's on these tapes. And so we've got to extend it further.

Because these tapes are so voluminous and there's so much information on these tapes that I believe this court is going to find very, very relevant, we need Mr. Dershowitz— Professor Der..howitz and Professor Uelman also involved. Because we anticipate any motion they may bring clearly relevant. And the question is, we don't want to pay— play, at this point, 13 or 14 hours of tapes. Maybe five or six hours, but certainly not 13 or 14. We'd like to narrow it down. In order to do that, if the Court pleases, we want to be able to share that with our colleagues, and we want to do a major brief spelling out the various points and the various relevance, and I think it'll

"PHYSICALLY CHALLENGED"

A journalist called me the other day from Washington, D.C. She said the high mucky-mucks of the disabled community were deciding on a new updated handle for handicapped people. She was calling up prominent disabled people to ask them what new term might be used. "You know," she said, "you all used to be referred to as *handicapped*. Next it was *physically challenged*. A few years ago it evolved to *person with a disability*."

This can't be real, I thought. The politically correct movement is still alive and well! "I don't know," I said. "Maybe *gimps*? Or how about *the maimed*?"

"Please, Mr. Callahan, I'm a big fan of your work, and I appreciate your humor, but I'm serious here. Do you have any suggestions I can use in my article?"

"I'm sorry," I said. "Let me think a minute!" My mind scrambled for a helpful suggestion! The *spiritually advantaged*? the *handicapable*? the *wheelchair-welded*? . . .

"Well, Mr. Callahan, are you there?"

"Yes," I said.

"Have you anything to offer?"

"Look," I said, "let me be honest with you. I do not think anyone will be able to come up with a term that is so freeing, so elevating, so warm and fuzzy that it will make me forget the grim reality of my circumstances and infuse me with confidence and self-esteem and propel me into a world of achievement and . . ."

A Matter of Taste

Dear Editor:

    I find humor in this drawing to be obviously lacking. In fact, it is rude and heartless in its presentation of an issue that is in no context a laughing matter. I am a registered nurse who's had many opportunities to witness how devastating a spinal cord injury is to the patient and his or her family. The cartoon depicting paralyzed people listening to a gospel song saying, *You'll never walk alone . . .* is tasteless. I am disgusted, not only that someone would draw this in an attempt at humor, but that you, as editors, would allow such garbage to be printed. I certainly hope the next time you review material for publication you will do so with at least one functioning neuron. I am sickened.

Michele D.
Oakland Park

Dear Editor:

Last year you printed a Callahan cartoon showing people in a church singing *You'll Never Walk Alone* and across the street was a hospital for people with spinal cord injuries. I had a good laugh over that one. In 1953, I was at Georgia Warm Springs Foundation for police rehabilitation. The woman in the next room played that song on her record player incessantly. It obviously gave her spiritual solace, but for me it was only a reminder of the facts of life. Callahan's cartoon made me realize how far I had come in acceptance and the ability to laugh at myself.

Remind your readers that Callahan is one of those unfortunates some readers seem to pity so much and his biggest fans are those who share his fate and we say: "Lighten up, you people."

Reba S.
Fort Lauderdale

Tropic, the Sunday magazine of
The Miami Herald
January 1992

August 2, 1994

John Callahan
c/o NobleWorks
Hoboken, New Jersey

Dear Mr. Callahan,

My late husband was a chiropractor for 42 years. He treated and helped many hundreds in the span of his career and was not able to help many as is often the case in all of the health care field. He was caring, ethical and competent.

If you had an unfortunate or unpleasant experience with a chiropractor that is a shame. Did you have? Is that why your greeting card "Famous Last Words" has slandered a whole profession? How thoughtless, mean-spirited and unfair of you!

Yours truly,

Rosalyn B.
Santa Barbara, California

July 24, 1992

Deborah Levin
Levin Represents
Venice, California

Dear Ms. Levin:

The members of the California Chiropractic Association noted
the uncomplimentary cartoon by Callahan, in the May edition
of the Santa Barbara Independent. . . . By calling a chiropractor
a quack, the cartoon is saying that chiropractors fraudulently
misrepresent their abilities and are unable to treat patients
effectively.

Chiropractic care is the second largest healing art in the world.
Chiropractic care emphasizes wellness and is a drug-free, non-
surgical approach to health care.

Best Regards and Health,

James E. Peterson, DC
CCA President

SURGERY

This morning Franny asked me if I've given any more thought to the surgeries I'm supposed to have. I hate it when she prods me on this matter. I'm supposed to undergo a hemorrhoid-reduction operation as well as some kind of procedure to blast out a couple of kidney stones. With a joke, I always skirt the subject in mock disgust. The truth is I am terrified of surgery at this time in my life. It's not actually the surgery, but it is the anesthetic part I'm afraid of. The idea of being chemically bludgeoned into unconsciousness seems hellish to me. It's like loss of all control, a slipping away, a kind of dying, but I can't very well request a priest there to read Psalm 23 to me as I'm pushed along.

I've had my share of major surgeries along this joyful path of quadriplegia. I'm no novice! I have no great fear that the surgeons will not be adept at the procedures they undertake. It is only the part about slipping away that horrifies me. I'm sure it's due to what I'm going through right now in therapy, a kind of power struggle deep in my subconscious or something. Lately, even my therapist has turned against me! He's been gently, but consistently, prodding me about recognizing my physical health needs. (I'm thinking of getting another therapist.)

Anyway, I've decided on a plan for dealing with the problem that might please all parties concerned. I will send a letter to my surgeon expressing the fact that I am willing to undergo the needed procedure, but only with a slightly altered method of anesthetic administration. I will request that the anesthesiologist purchase one of those tranquilizer rifles that game wardens use to put big-game animals to sleep. I will suggest this doctor simply lie in wait for me somewhere around town and shoot me on a day when I'm going about my business and blissfully unaware of anything. My body could then be transported to the hospital for the needed surgery.

All I'm really asking is to be treated as humanely as one of our creatures of the wild. If a Kodiak bear can be gently dispatched to unconsciousness, why can't I? Must I rent a bear's costume and run around in the woods to achieve this end?

THE POPE DIGS MADONNA

CALLAHAN

BLASPHEMY!

Dear Editor:

I was stunned when I opened the Jan. 19 Tropic and saw the insulting and irreverent depiction of Pope John Paul II, adorned, apparently, with Madonna's latest breast-cover. . . .

This is the type of cartoon one would expect to find in some establishment-bashing underground publication, not in a feature magazine of one of the foremost newspapers in the United States. Did you find it amusing? If so, you and anyone else who enjoyed it must be either extremely ignorant or hard-up for laughs.

Pope John Paul II has spent most of his term as head of the church urging the peoples of every nation to holiness, to service of God and to love of neighbor. He has particularly been outspoken with regard to family morals, respect of human life, and purity in human relations. The Madonna to whom he turns his attention is Mary, the mother of Christ and our mother. I believe there is an oblique slur of her involved in this cartoon. Contrast her with the Madonna who seemingly misuses the great talents God has given her to the detriment of the young.

Mary is the model for all women: pure and chaste (yes, it is possible to have these virtues today, married or unmarried), humble and loving, willing to sacrifice herself for others, faithful and trusting of God. . . . If the editors have any concrete and worthy reason for having printed that Callahan cartoon, they best write it down so they won't forget what it is when they are called to explain themselves to the "Executive Editor" of the "Final Edition."

Dale K.
Plantation

Tropic, the Sunday magazine of *The Miami Herald*
April 1994

Books & Religion

A QUARTERLY REVIEW

June 25, 1992

Deborah Levin
Levin Represents
Venice, California

Dear Ms. Levin,

Callahan's vision of the world is one that needs to be seen by as many people
as possible. Religious types especially.

Yours,

Deborah G. Bly
Associate Editor

NUN KICKING HABIT

July 2, 1992

Levin Represents
Venice, CA

Dear Sirs,

Recently I purchased a group of postcards by John Callahan, using subjects not usually used for humor. They have made a BIG HIT with all my intelligent friends. I gave them the supreme test! I sent a set to my sister who is a nun with the Order of Notre Dame. Sister Jeanne Marie will be 79 years old on December 15th. She thought these cards were unique and clever and humorous without offense.

Thank you so much for appreciating the clever and original talent of John Callahan. This is "human humor." Best wishes for many sales!

Sincerely and thank you again,

Mildred S.
Washington, D.C.

NORDSTROM PISS OCCURRENCE

Another living hell!

I was downtown the other day when I heard a melodic female voice call out my name. I slowed my wheelchair down and looked back to see a beautiful young woman standing in front of the Nordstrom department store. "Are you Callahan the Cartoonist?" she asked breathlessly.

"Why, yes I am," I said, my heart pounding. She had green eyes, high cheekbones, and thick brown hair styled in a sexy blunt cut.

"Oh, my God! I'm your biggest fan. I've got all your books and I saw you on *60 Minutes* and everything!" She seemed irresistibly girlish as she squealed with delight. I stole a quick glance at her nubile figure, large breasts spilling over a low-cut black dress with shapely legs rising out of red high-heeled shoes.

"You're too kind," I said, as I struggled to catch my breath and appear relaxed. (What I really felt like doing was holding a pistol to my temple and pulling the trigger with her gorgeous form as the final image I saw in the world as the death-blackness overtook my vision and I slumped over dead before her with a slight smile on my dead and bloody face.)

"Isn't it true Robin Williams is going to do a movie about you?"

"Well, yes, he did buy the option. What do you do?" I said, struggling to put the focus on her for a bit.

"Oh, I'm a student at Lewis and Clark Law School," she said. "I hope to graduate this year."

"You look too young for law school," I said, when suddenly a loud splashing sound was heard below my wheelchair. "Oh, my God!" I thought. "It can't be! It simply can't BE!" The look of horror in her eyes confirmed my fear. It had happened. My worst fear had come true. The splashing sound continued. The seconds ticked away, during which time my entire life passed before my eyes.

Yes, the splashing sound was urine, my urine. The peg had slipped out of the tube of my leg bag and now the urine was splashing loudly upon the pavement below my chair. Our eyes met and she looked like Jackie Kennedy did when her husband's head had been blown to pieces before her. Still the urine splashed. . . .

"Oh, I'd like to go to law school too. . . ." I struggled instinctively to talk over the awful splashing. "I . . . I . . ." But it was no use. The splashing was finally quieting, and turning into a gentle tickle. "I . . . I . . ."

My brain was on fire with a hundred different emotions. How could this have happened? What kind of God would allow a thing like this to happen? I felt my ears burning with a rage that swept through my entire being. "Why me?" I thought. "Why me?" But I kept talking. "I . . . I . . . had a cousin who was a lawyer. I . . . I . . ." I could not talk away the horror of the situation. Her eyes were still wide with fear and embarrassment. "Oh, deliver me from the moment," I prayed, "Holy Mother of Sorrows. . . ."

I wanted to leave, to drive my wheelchair away, but I couldn't. If I moved my chair, she would see the puddle of urine below me. I was stuck. Finally she said she had to catch a bus and she walked away. As soon as she was gone, I drove away quickly, never daring to look back at the fateful pool of bodily waste that surely glistened for all to see in the noonday sun, upon the fancy brick entrance to the glitzy department store.

Yes, the puddle of urine would stand. Stand for all to see as a a testimony to the farce and the joke that my life truly is.

The Presbyterian Hospital in the City of New York

Columbia-Presbyterian Medical Center, New York, NY 10032-3784

November 3, 1993

Levin Represents
Deborah Levin
Santa Monica, California

Dear Ms. Levin:

Please send us information on your collection of John Callahan tee shirts, mugs, condoms, wheel chair cushions and whatever else you have.

Mr. Callahan has a following among the night shift nurses in the Emergency Room of Columbia Presbyterian Medical Center in New York City. We laugh at his cartoons <u>and</u> we find them funny.

We are also admirers of "Jenny," Mr. Callahan's rehab. nurse, since none of us have ever met a nurse who cares for her patients in quite the way she did.

So please send us your information and tell Mr. Callahan to stop by if he is ever in New York City after midnight.

Sincerely,

Maggie D.	Irene V.	Lorraine S.
Marti K.	Mary K.	Pat H.
Barbi W.	Wendy W.	Rafi P.
Gary P.	Marge G.	Margaret D.

POTTY-CHAIR

I'm on the potty-chair now, and I pray things will go easily. I'm in the middle of my huge country kitchen, with shaded windows all around. On the desk in front of me is my drawing pad. My phone, my harmonica, and my fax machine are nearby. I'm completely naked and ready to begin my workday. I feel like a young bullfighter, stoking courage and fighting off feelings of dread. I wonder if people know I have created the majority of my work while seated upon the potty-chair. I don't think I could bear it if I was asked to draw while on TV.

On my left is my Diet Coke, which, of course, is half full, and on my right is a copy of today's newspaper's classified section. I will commence my day as always by searching the ads for a suitable dog to purchase. A sinking feeling always overtakes me as I circle the several possibilities that spring before me: "4-year-old St. Bernard, loving and obedient," "6-year-old Labrador, housebroken and loyal," "2-year-old Lhasa apso" . . . But this time, my heart begins to pound, and my fingers tremble with the excitement of the chase. Aha! These are very real possibilities; these dogs are definite possibilities! I'm really onto something here! Where is my Diet Coke! Ha ha! The paper is bursting with possibilities!

Dogs, dogs, dogs! Wonderful, loyal, obedient dogs. Dogs imbued with an almost transcendental sense of loyalty. Things will all be different when I own one of these dogs! The sinking feeling is all but a memory as my quaking hand lurches for the phone. "Hello, I'm calling about the six-year-old Lab? Do you still have him? Oh, you do? Would it be possible to send the four hundred dollars over immediately with my cabdriver?"

The sight of a rubber glove behind me jerks me to a hellish reality. Bill cackles mockingly at me, and I hear the cackles of the ten thousand attendants before him, all of whom stood snapping their rubber gloves on in the same spot in my huge kitchen. "Yes. Yes, *of course* it would be more realistic for me to come look at the dog before I purchased him! You must think I'm silly!"

Bill begins to work his grisly magic, and my eyes fall upon the sketch pad he has placed upon my knees. The snow-white page also mocks me as I furtively bite the pen. Dreams of the perfect dog have slipped away into oblivion as life's bone-crushing harshness presents itself. Deborah Levin's cartoon is due, and it's due soon! It must be finished, funny, and baked, all by ten-thirty this morning.

The kitchen is cold as the carping continues. "Take a break, Bill. And oh, on your way out, could you just click on the radio?" I couch the words in as nonchalant a way as I can, but it is no use. Bill is hip to my scheme!

"But Deborah Levin doesn't think it's good for you to . . ."

"Never mind what Deborah Levin says," I say. I hesitate as Bill's gloved fingers hover tentatively above the radio knob. Time seems to slow down like a dream as I sit naked in my huge kitchen and with Bill on the cusp of my indecision.

The moment I dread is upon me. Where is my Diet Coke? Snickers barks from the sitting room. Bill twitches nervously, tapping his foot and resetting his baseball cap. In my mind's eye, I see Deborah Levin standing in miniature upon my shoulder. She is wearing heels and dressed in a tasteful navy suit, sporting designer sunglasses, left hand holding a rolling pin. She whispers in my ear, "He's cynical and negative, and my mother thinks you've been in a depression ever since you've been listening to him!"

Upon my other shoulder, also in miniature, stands the K-Man with a tiny beer in each hand. He leans tipsily toward my ear, whispering, "Go ahead and listen to him. Fuck all these sunken-chested liberals!"

My mind is spinning; my thoughts are careening out of control. I must make a decision. My Diet Coke is empty . . . what to do? . . . what to do? A monolithic ambivalence has come over me, as I sit here naked upon my potty-chair, in my kitchen. "Turn it on, Bill," I utter weakly through the maelstrom of my calm. "Turn it on!"

Bill hits the switch, and the genie is freed from the bottle: "Hello, everyone along the fruited plain, it's Rush Limbaugh on the EIB Network!"

THE ALZHEIMER HOEDOWN

...allemande right and please be deft, NOW return to the girl that you just left!

CALLAHAN

September 6, 1994

Nobleworks
Hoboken, New Jersey
Attention: John Callahan

Dear Mr. Callahan,

I am writing to complain about a postcard I purchased from the Towson State
University Book Store in Towson, Maryland, last year.

When I read this postcard, I was very upset and would never think of purchas-
ing it. Several weeks later I was assigned a report to do for my health 101 class
and I chose to do Alzheimer's disease and how it affects the patient's family
members. As I was thinking of a creative way to present this topic, I remem-
bered the postcard I saw in the bookstore. I then hesitantly went back and purchased it.

I think that it is horrible that I had to purchase such a horrible thing and to add
to your profits. I think you have a warped sense of humor that in my view is
anything but funny. I have kept this item just in case I am assigned a similar
project in my last year of college. I will continue to use it to show how unaware
people are and to explain what Alzheimer's disease really is.

Sincerely,

Michelle C.

ALZ EIMER'S ®
ASSOCIATION
Someone to Stand By You.

September 20, 1991

Mr. John Callahan
Mrs. Deborah Levin
Venice, California

Dear Mr. Callahan and Mrs. Levin:

In a recent edition of *The Riverfront Times,* you printed a cartoon depicting a square dance as an "Alzheimer's Hoedown." Several of our family caregivers of AD victims contacted our office to voice their outrage at your insensitivity. . . .

No doubt, AD people will make foolish mistakes and not be able to use good judgment. However, this loss of cognitive function is a result of a disease process. AD victims should be treated with dignity and compassion—not ridicule. . . .

I suggest you owe an apology to the Alzheimer's families throughout the country.

Sincerely,

Kathleen Higley
Executive Director

THE MENTAL HOSPITAL CHOIR

January 1, 1994

Mr. John Callahan
c/o Levin Represents
Noble Works
Hoboken, New Jersey

Dear Mr. Callahan:

I am quite a big fan of your work and believe that you have probably done more for mental health than all of us psychologists put together! It would be wonderful if you could share some of you philosophy with our group at one of our continuing education events. I wonder whether public speaking/lecturing is part of your typical venue, and whether you come to the West Coast often.

If you would be so kind as to let me know whether this is a possibility, and what fees might be involved, I will present a proposal to our Board of Directors.

Thanking you in advance for your response, and thanking you for your humor.

Sincerely,

Alison E. Stanley, Ph.D.
President

ALLIANCE for the MENTALLY ILL of CONTRA COSTA

December 4, 1996

John Callahan
NobleWorks
Hoboken, New Jersey

Dear Mr. Callahan:

Our group was extremely disappointed with your Christmas card featuring
"The Mental Christmas Choir." There is nothing humorous about mental illness, or the phenomenon of hearing voices, or staying in a psychiatric ward,
and cards like these perpetuate the stigma against people with brain disorders.

I am enclosing the brochure "Information for Writers," put out by the National
Alliance for the Mentally Ill to explain more specifically which references are
derogatory and why.

Thank you for your attention.

Sincerely,

Karen Cohen
Public Relations Chair

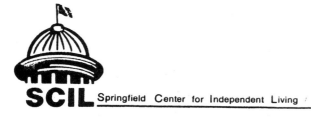

SCIL Springfield Center for Independent Living

July 21, 1994

Levin Represents
Deborah Levin
Santa Monica, California

Dear Ms. Levin,

The Springfield Center for Independent Living is a non-profit service and advocacy organization controlled by persons with disabilities. Our mission is to change perceptions and attitudes about persons with disabilities, and to change the service systems that create and foster dependence.

Enough of that. We love John Callahan. We want to meet him. We want others to meet him. We want him to come to Springfield, to honor us as our keynote and special guest at our annual meeting. We expect that the audience will be a statewide one, given his popularity.

We look forward to hearing from you at your earliest convenience, and to having the opportunity to personally thank John Callahan for being on the planet.

Sincerely yours,

Pete Roberts   Kevin Cain, Co-Chair,
Executive Director   Human Resources Committee

September 14, 1994

Dear John Callahan,

You're sick and twisted . . . and I really like that in a
man.

Besides which, you push every button I've got. I'm
Irish and an alcoholic and I'm trying to quit (the alco-
hol, not the Irishness). My older brother was adopted
and then—ta da!—I showed up. My best friend is a
Catholic priest with AIDS, and we both love your cartoons. And since reading your autobiography—well,
frankly, Toots, I've got a ground-floor apartment.

You don't need to worry much about not being able to
feel your balls—you've definitely got 'em, more so
than any man I've met in a long time.

Many thanks for being such an outrageous bastard
and unleashing yourself on the world as is.

Sincerely,

Dhyan R.
San Francisco

LETTER TO THE EDITOR
CALLAHAN REDUX

Dear Editor:

   I realize that Callahan's macabre sense of humor generates many letters and angry comments. His insensitivity is always under fire. Perhaps it is time that you re-run this cartoonist's personal history. I have never forgotten your article on him when you first introduced his work.

   I respect the fact that he may want to be seen as a simple commentator on human foibles, but I think that his unique background gives him the right to be also seen as a very special survivor against major odds that most of us can only applaud and respect.

   I love his mordant humor and his evil eye. Believe me, there are many of us out here who just wait for the next Callahan entry.

Esther H.
Plantation

Tropic, the Sunday magazine of
The Miami Herald
May 31, 1992

Dear Editor:

In our very serious endeavor to heal ourselves and our planet, we left humor out of the pie. I don't feel like I'm laughing at any one group that Callahan may be pointing his pencil at. Instead, I'm laughing at the humanness in all of us that makes it OK to have good intentions and still fall flat on our faces.

Donna B.
Los Angeles

Los Angeles Times Magazine
December 1990

ACLU OREGON

AMERICAN CIVIL LIBERTIES UNION

29 July 1991

John Callahan
Portland, Oregon

Dear John:

It is a thrill for me to write this letter to you.

The ACLU Foundation of Oregon Free Expression Award is given annually. The award recognizes a supporter for First Amendment rights of free expression in Oregon who has demonstrated remarkable personal courage or creative vision in upholding these rights.

Your nomination and affirmation was made on the basis of your history of facing challenge to artistic and intellectual freedom with courage in the face of dissenting opinion.

I spoke with a wide range of people in researching your nomination. They spoke highly of your personal integrity, your very specialized creative genius and your willingness to face controversial issues and behaviors in your writing and your cartoons, regardless of the marketability these pieces may have.

The award will be presented to you at a reception on Thursday, September 26th, 5:30 p.m. at the Portland Art Museum. Please invite any guests you would like to attend. I would be happy to send invitations to them.

I must tell you how much I admire you. I am really looking forward to meeting you in person.

Yours truly,

Janet Arenz
Associate Director, Education

SCORING BIG

Here are my first cartoon sales. The checks are in the order in which they were received.

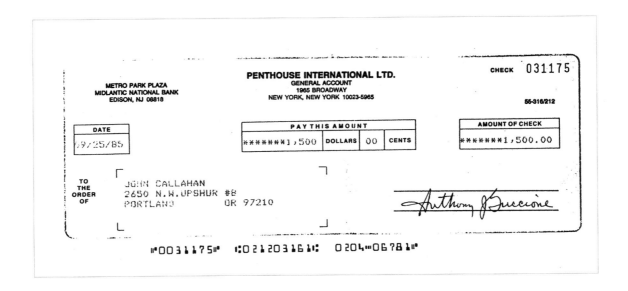

L.F.P. INC D/B/A CHIC MAG.
2029 CENTURY PK EAST STE.3800
LOS ANGELES, CA 90067

FIRST BEVERLY BANK
CENTURY CITY BRANCH
Los Angeles, California 90067

413230

90-3798
1222

DATE: 02/12/86

PAY ONE HUNDRED DOLLARS AND ZERO CENTS $********100.00

To
The
Order
Of

CALLAHAN, JOHN
2650 NW UPSHUR # 3
PORTLAND, OR

AUTHORIZED SIGNATURE

NOT VALID OVER $2,500.00

AUTHORIZED SIGNATURE

⑈413230⑈ ⑆1222379841⑆ 862⑈0066615⑈

THE NEW YORKER

25 WEST 43rd STREET
NEW YORK 10036

1-23
210

CHECK NO 27017

NEW YORK·N·Y February 27, 19 86

PAY TO THE ORDER OF John M. Callahan $ 150.00 ************

THE NEW YORKER MAGAZINE, INC.

This check represents payment in respect
of the following Work:
AH-388 "There, there, dear. It's..." (Idea Payment)

AUTHORIZED SIGNATURE

⑆021000238⑆ 108 01 608⑈

WITHOUT A PADDLE

The other day after my shower, Bill helped me swing back into bed. He then heard a loud noise in the basement and ran down the stairs to investigate. After a few minutes, I began to wonder what had happened to him. As the minutes ticked by, it occurred to me that I was completely naked, sprawled across my bed with one leg dangling unflatteringly off the edge, completely powerless to move a muscle. I began to feel chilled, then somewhat vulnerable. "Bill, where are you?" I called out, entreaty in my voice.

No answer. Irritation began to replace vulnerability. Irritation escalated when I noticed that the screen door down the hall was propped wide open. Anyone arriving at my house would immediately see me lying there in all my paralysis. "Bill!" I shouted, "Bill!" As I grew more and more desperate, my voice croaked with anger. "GODDAMMIT! BILL, WHERE THE HELL ARE YOU!"

I felt a burning in my chest, and a burning in my stomach. I was beginning to panic. I wanted Bill to return and arrange my helpless body into the proper position immediately! Panic was rising. But why was I getting so upset? Bill would return soon, no doubt, and all would be well. Why was I reacting with such a level of terror?

It was as if I was running away from something I was terrified of. Some sort of monster. Something deep inside I could not face. I closed my eyes. I took a deep breath. I tried to calm myself. I wanted to find out what it was that always so terrified me.

I'd been in this situation many times in the last twenty-three years, but it seemed to be getting worse with time. I was always surprised, and I was always annoyed for not being used to it by now. How many times would I suffer anew? When will I ever get used to the idea that I simply cannot move my limbs?

It was as if I'd never really faced it. I always found some way to distract myself from that fact, force my mind to think about something else.

The tears of rage were building as my torso hummed with the heat of fear and anger. I was reaching a panic crescendo, but another part of me seemed to be standing off and watching more objectively. A part of me that had spent seventeen years in AA struggling to "turn things over to a higher power." A part of me that had spent years in therapy "trying to experience my feelings." A part of me that really had been progressing in serenity and self-fulfillment.

That part of me now seemed to be saying, "Okay, you've faced lots of dragons in the past two decades; now you're ready to face the main monster. Why not stop running from it for once? Why not face it and see what its nature is?"

I decided to take the "leap." As I drew a deep breath, I tried to focus. But the hurricane of panic was still roaring in my mind and body, and I went down, down, down with the maelstrom. There was great resistance, my mind trying desperately to distract me from the real fear in my being. "Don't look! Don't look! Think about something else! Think about where Bill could be! Think about how you're gonna scream at him. Think about when he comes back! Think about the control you're trying to reestablish!" Control! Control! That was it!

I recognized the panic, took more deep breaths, and tried to let myself feel. I was in battle with myself. One part of me was battling to recover something. Another part of me was protecting me at all costs. What was the nature of these feelings? I struggled to stay with it. I was getting closer . . . closer . . . It was a feeling of ultimate terror, a terror of being out of control, of having no control. A feeling of having all my power and control taken from me. I realized this little by little as I recognized this maelstrom of thought and physical sensation trying to distract me. I let myself experience the feelings. I recognized that I was indeed feeling the horror of . . .

But something deep inside was saying, "Trust me. Remember how you faced it once before when you dropped that bottle so many years before? Give up. Let go . . . come home. Stop trying to control everything . . . you can trust me . . . you can let go of the edges and drop into the unknown." At this point the horrors kicked up again. Turn away! Think of something else. Run! Run!!

But I hung on through it, and I let my grip loosen. I said, "Geronimo," and I fell. Peace! Peace! That's what's at the bottom of this horror? Peace? And with the peace that old familiar presence was there. It seemed to be saying to me, "Yes, I understand. I am aware of everything you go through. I understand all you feel."

But *this* presence was not holding a calculator in one hand adding up the intensity of my sufferings to be submitted later to some god in order to determine the value of my final reward.

This is what I'd been taught was the nature of suffering, that one gets a higher or lower place in heaven according to how much he suffered on earth. "Offer it up," chirped the nuns. A schoolchild smashed his fingers in his desk and squeaked in pain.

Instead the experience I was now having seemed to be telling me that my reward was given in the moment at hand. The reward was understanding, enlightenment. The understanding that my suffering was only just resistance to the truth. The truth that there is higher, loving intelligence that takes care of all things! It knows best what my needs are and how best to fulfill them. That I can always let go at any earthly moment and drop into this peace, and get the right direction.

I realized at this point that maybe there *was* no future to look to. Maybe there was no past to gaze back upon. Maybe this peaceful moment I was in is all the time that exists. It occurred to me that time just could be one of these pesky little illusions in this peaceful state; everything seemed to be the way it was all supposed to be. It was all for some reason, some plan. Strangely, there seemed to be a further feeling that I'd had a hand in creating my odd life's circumstance. More than this I cannot say, because the feeling is so very vague.

Bill finally arrived back at my bedside. "Sorry. The dog got her head caught behind the washing machine!"

"That's all right?" I said, grateful to have him back. But one final warning to the reader: Don't try this at HOME!

One final letter. (I can't quite place the name, but I have the letter framed!)

THE WHITE HOUSE
WASHINGTON

April 23, 1993

John Callahan
Venice, California

Dear John:

Thank you for your great card and for sending
the article and the original drawing. You were
kind to think of me.

I appreciate your offer of help with my humor,
but don't you think I'm funny enough already?
Seriously, I do appreciate it, and I may just
take you up on it sometime soon.

Sincerely,

Bill Clinton

CALLAHAN

K·MAN

K-Man is my best friend. We met twelve years ago when he stepped out from a seedy restaurant, wearing a greasy chef's hat, and introduced himself. Each of us thought the other was a prick, and we have been soul mates ever since.

K-Man is a distinctive soul, looking basically like a cross between Broderick Crawford and Sebastian Cabot. Barrel-chested and bloated, his torso weighs heavily upon the thin mosquito legs God gave him. He walks on the outside of his feet in painful pronation, reminiscent of the trained chimps on the Ed Sullivan show. His head is large, and his face ("I've got a face like a canned ham," he often exclaims) glows with the heightened blood pressure of the late-stage alcoholic. His features are fine, almost aristocratic, but are somehow lost in the fleshy expanse of his massive countenance.

Here is a drawing I made of him ten years ago when we first started hanging out:

K-Man and I have very similar backgrounds: Catholic school, heavy drinking, a love for dogs, and dead mothers. Our main tie is through our sense of humor. It's like a blueprint shared by both our minds. We've shared many adventures together. Here are some of them for you chronicled in cartoon form:

When I first met K-Man, he had just moved to Portland from Jersey. He spent lots of time "informing" me about how provincial Portland was compared with New Jersey.

"THE BIG MAC ATTACK"

K-Man has always been carousing around the streets. This is a true story about K-Man irritating a dog. (The main motivation behind K-Man's ill-fated persistence was Budweiser, I'm afraid.)

And now here's a documentary of our first movie together. (I'm not proud of it!)

K-Man is a big meat eater. (As I always tell the waitresses.) He has an all-consuming passion for steak; his consumption of it is both barbaric and ritualistic.

K-Man is also adept at selecting good Chinese food. Here is a true story of the hapless lout's bad luck with the fortune cookies.

"SWEET AND SOUR PUKE"

I. K-MAN GOES TO CHINESE RESTAURANT...

II. ORDERS A BOWL OF EGG FLOWER SOUP.

III. FEELS QUEASY AND CALLS CAB...

CLAB COMING SOON, MISAH KLAMAN!

IV. K-MAN PUKES OUT DOOR OF CAB WHEN CAB STOPS AT A LIGHT...

V. CRAWLS TO HIS APARTMENT DOOR...

VI. HEAVES GUTS INTO TOILET...

VII. K-MAN MUST SIT FOR A LONG TIME IN MISERY ON CAN...

VIII. HE ONLY FEELS WORSE, AND BEGINS TO SEE STARS...

IX. FINALLY K-MAN LOSES CONSCIOUSNESS AND FALLS INTO SHOWER.

150

Actually, people who know him would be shocked that such a brilliant personality would have had such a tough beginning. It is a little-known fact that during K-Man's childhood he suffered like a pig in hell.

The K-Ster in a secret moment.

No one believes this one, but it happened!

"K-MAN'S ROADKILL-REALIZATION"

I. K-MAN DRINKING IN "WIMPY'S" BAR AND GRILL...

II. HEARS WOMAN'S SCREAMS COMING FROM KITCHEN...
EEEE! EEE...

III. SCREAMS CONTINUE...
EEEE!!!

IV. K-MAN DECIDES TO INVESTIGATE THE SITUATION...

V. AS THE K-MAN ENTERS THE KITCHEN HE EXPECTS TO SEE THE COOK MOLESTING A WAITRESS...

VI. INSTEAD, THE K-MAN FINDS THE COOK STANDING ALONE WITH A NUMBER TEN CAN OF TOMATO PASTE WITH BLOOD DRIPPING FROM IT...

VII. AS K-MAN LOOKS FURTHER HE SPIES A BLOODY, DEAD POSSUM ON THE FLOOR IN THE CORNER...

VIII. K-MAN INSTANTLY REALIZES THE COOK HAS BEATEN THE POSSUM TO DEATH WITH THE NUMBER TEN CAN OF TOMATO PASTE!!!

IX. AMID THE CLATTER OF CUPS AND SAUCERS NOTHING IS REVEALED, ONLY A DARK TWINKLING REMAINS IN THE GLEAMING EYES OF THE K-MAN!

As close as we are, there are times when K-Man needs to spend time alone. Here is how K-Man rejects me each Sunday:

All in all, K-Man has been a great friend and a special inspiration in my life. It is here that he has peeled the paint off the walls of my bathroom on many occasions with rancid, beer-soaked bowel movements. But those are the wages of friendship with a happy-go-lucky Irishman.

I was disheartened when I could not get the following cartoons published in even the *National Paralytic Newsletter*. I sent the rejection letter back to them with a note saying that I wouldn't want any of my work published in a magazine with such a stupid name anyway.

CATALOG OF ADAPTIVE EQUIPMENT FOR THE HANDICAPPED

CARTOONIST JOHN CALLAHAN
SHARES HIS LATEST INVENTIONS
(inspired by his own disability)

A new 'balloon holder' for quadruple amputees frees the mouth of the user for talking.

$2.00

Why did I have to yawn, my balloon got away!

ooo

Hey, I can open my mouth and my balloon doesn't get away!!

Before

after

a new piece of adaptive equipment that solves the age-old problem of in-accessibility...
$ 140.00
...take it easy, buddy, we've got the carpenter on the phone!!!

The 'Bullhorn-a-plenty' to aid handicapped with cooking...
$10.95
Please help me! I'm hungry, but I'm para-lyzed and can't cook!!

Border Collies, trained to herd sheep, are now used to guide the blind.

$270.00

adaptive equipment for paralyzed stand-up comics $18.95

(fake arrows through knees)

... just rolled in from Vegas, boy, are my arms sore...

A cuckoo clock for the deaf with little hands that pop out and sign the words coo - coo.

 $37.00

Hmm... coo-coo!

Contact lenses
for the blind: $55.00

before

after

$18.50
I invented the ALL
new 'crawl alert' for
the the forgetful para-
plegic... like me!
I'll meet you at the office, Bill, I've forgotten my chair again!
(paraplegic's stomach srapes sidewalk act-
ivating 'crawl-alert')
Beep Beep
Beep Beep

MIDDLE-AGE CADNESS

If one more woman completely ignores me on the street, I think I'm going to turn around, rev up my wheelchair, and crash into her headlong while screaming obscenities at the top of my lungs! What in the hell has happened! I can't stand it anymore! I'm gonna go crazy! Every single member of the female gender ignores me as if I wasn't even there. I don't care if I'm on the trendy sidewalk a few blocks from my house, at the airport terminal, or in a crowded restaurant with waitresses taking my order. It's like I'm invisible! How can a waitress take my order without making eye contact? Sometimes I get panicky and begin to actively *try* to elicit a response from a woman passing me by. I'll straighten my shoulders, stick out my chest, suck in my stomach, and smile. Nothing!

The feeling I experience is a combination of panic, sadness, self-revulsion, self-pity, rage, and nausea. It's not that I think I'm so good-looking—I know I'm not!!! It's true when I was fifteen years younger, I was considered to be ruggedly handsome, with a somewhat charismatic presence. I had just cleaned up from alcoholism, and I was attending Portland State University. It's true I was thirty pounds lighter in addition to the fifteen years younger. It's also true that I, more than most men, craved the attention of women, especially in the form of casual flirting. (My therapist believes I was sexually molested by an adult female outside my home when I was a small child and therefore must play cut this endless pattern of attention-seeking from women.) Anyway, for whatever reason, I enjoyed a level of female attention and companionship that was considered to be unusual. I was known as a lady's man, a hunk, a pussy-magnet. And whenever I met anyone new, she would inevitably say, "Every time I see you, you've always got a beautiful girl with you!"

I used to cruise around the the streets or halls of the college, just to catch the eye of the ladies. Sometimes I'd get a smile, or a look, sometimes not. It was like a sport for me. Round and round the downtown streets I'd roll, flirting my day away. The more attention I'd get, the greater my high. Sometimes I'd even receive notes from strangers saying, "You smiled at me downtown last Tuesday. Would you like to meet me for coffee?" Similarly, my phone answering machine might have a sweet voice lilting with a like invitation. My male friends couldn't believe it. "Wow, I've got to break my neck too!" K-Man used to exclaim. "Maybe *I* would score some broads!"

Yes, it was a pussy parade, and I enjoyed every minute of it. I don't know exactly what day it began to change, or just when it all began to cease, but it did and now I find myself *completely* bewildered. K-Man says, "It's Darwinism." Bonedog says, "It's middle age." And Franny says, "It's about time!" I suppose they're all correct. Middle age has settled in.

It's frustrating 'cause I don't feel that much older. Inside I still feel eighteen. I feel like I'm being dragged backward down the hall by the age police and I'm screaming, "I didn't do it! I'm not guilty!"

I feel this overwhelming denial of the facts. I still feel young—trapped in this wrinkly costume, a victim of hideous, selfish deeds I must now pay for as in a grotesque *Outer Limits* episode. Try as I might to accept the years, I cannot shake this feeling of youngness. I feel like I have one foot in *high school,* and one foot in *the grave.* I want to charge down the sidewalk shrieking, "It's me! It's really me under these wrinkles! It's John Callahan! It's only a mistake—it's really *me*!! I imagine the neighbors looking out their windows, shaking their heads in pity. "Poor bastard, he did the exact same thing when he became paralyzed!"

I've heard about the famous "midlife crisis" all my life. It's meaningless 'til you experience it personally. It's the classic transition of a young man to a more mature, wizened man. Of a man who considers his Corvette a "smooth-runnin' system," to a man who considers his Corvette a "life-support system."

K-Man always scolds me for my constant lamentations. "You're becoming middle-aged—big deal! Why do you let it bother you!!!

I was trying to relax in bed the other night when I heard on the radio that it was Rush Limbaugh's forty-fifth birthday. I sat up in horror! I'm the same age as Rush Limbaugh? But that can't be!! Rush Limbaugh is *ancient*. Rush Limbaugh is *middle-aged*! (But so am I!) Wait a minute, "I'm boyish and youthful—Rush Limbaugh was *born* middle-aged!"

Back and forth I go in my mind as I struggle to process the incongruent facts. Often I end in an anxiety attack, and I have to watch the Christian TV network until I'm calm enough to fall back into sleep.

My dreams are tortured too! Last night I dreamt that I was rolling down the street stopping every woman and carefully explaining to her that though she had not noticed me on *this* occasion, there *was* a time not long ago when she would have paid heavy money to have caught my eye.

All in all, this middle-age deal is major league! But I've been through a lot of difficulty in my life. Surely I can get through this. In fact, I actually feel like I might be making a little headway after all. I've been hiding in my bedroom for three days, but today I'm girding my loins and I am once again heading down to take my chances on the boulevard. I will once again roll bravely up and down the sidewalk and take my middle-age medicine. Once again I will endure the myriad faces of the women who pass me by, ignoring me. I will drink from this bitter cup and will bear up like a man. I will accept my fate, though in my heart I hold the tiniest pearl of hope, the meagerest fantasy. In my mind I see the lone figure of a woman standing curiously atop a tall building.

As I watch, she raises a bullhorn to her lips and calls out in a loud voice: "Okay, ladies! Everyone can stop pretending to ignore John Callahan now! The gag's over!" Suddenly, before my tearful eye, I see the hundreds of women up and down the street turn at once as they burst into tears of mirth. They gather around me squealing and giggling. One after another they hug me, saying, "We really had you fooled, huh?"

The nightmare is over, I thought. Finally!

CALLAHAN

"Let me put it this way. The nurse has lost your clothes..."

OLDER WOMEN GETTING PREGNANT...

PAMPERS

DEPENDS

GROCE.
STOR

CALLAHAN

I've always had an obsession with Humpty Dumpty. I relate to his cockiness and of course his ignominious demise. This strip was about as popular as a pay toilet in a diarrhea ward.

HUMPTY DUMPTY
(THE REAL STORY)
by JOHN CALLAHAN

172

MOVING TO THE LEFT

Whenever a stranger approaches me on the street, he will always do something very odd. He will begin by standing directly in front of me, but very quickly, usually shortly after the perfunctory verbal salutations, he will begin to move to my immediate left or right side. This forces me to turn my head unnaturally and painfully sideways to continue eye contact with him as we converse.

After a few moments of straining my neck in this position, I naturally begin to turn my chair slowly around to face the person more directly and relieve my neck. To my horror, the person begins moving farther to my left to counter my attempt. Every time I turn left to face them, they move in unison to maintain their position beside me. Faster and faster I turn; faster and faster the person sidesteps. I simply cannot gain on them. It's like trying to focus your eyes upon the blue dot that hovers in your periphery after a camera flash.

After a while, it begins to really irritate me. It becomes a matter of power and control. I decide to take ultimate control of the situation; I jam the joystick to the hilt and the chair lurches powerfully to the left. It's no use; the enemy has already anticipated the maneuver, and is literally running to maintain his position beside my elbow. The conversation never misses a beat as this dizzy dance continues! "I first saw your cartoon in *Penthouse*. . . ."

Round and round we go. I feel like I need Dramamine! Finally, I give in and stop moving my chair. Once again I must succumb to my fate of having to turn my head uncomfortably around sideways to face my conversationalist. Life is full of small surrenderings.

CALLAHAN

Here's a piece I wrote ten years ago. At the time I thought it was humorous, incisive, and poignant. Looking back, I now realize it was humorous, incisive, poignant, and sucked whale dicks. See for yourself.

ONCE UPON WELFARE

BY JOHN CALLAHAN

WELFARE PROVIDED AN ATTENDANT FOR ME. HER NAME WAS ADRIENNE. SHE HELPED ME WITH THE THINGS I COULDN'T DO FOR MYSELF.

ADRIENNE WAS GOOD
FOR ME AND SHE LOVED
MY CAT LIZZY, THOUGH
LIZZY WAS DEATHLY A-
FRAID OF HER.

SOMETIMES, WHEN I BECAME
DEPRESSED ABOUT FINANCES,
ADRIENNE, WHO WAS A CHRIST-
IAN, WOULD READ ME A
BIBLE VERSE...

...and Job snivelled unto God...

ONCE IN A WHILE WELFARE
GAVE AWAY FREE CHEESE,
BUT THE AMOUNT WAS SO
MINIMAL THAT WE USED IT TO
CATCH RATS TO EAT!

WHEN REAGAN TOOK OFFICE
THE WELFARE BUDGET SHRUNK
EVEN MORE. ADRIENNE AND
I FOUND A LESS EXPENSIVE
LIVING SPACE...

I BEGAN THINKING OF
WAYS TO BRING IN MORE
CASH TO MAKE ENDS MEET.

183

184

185

THESE IDEAS DIDN'T SEEM WORKABLE
TO ME, SO I TURNED TO THE ONLY
TALENT I POSSESSED — DRAWING.

I MADE A FEW BUCKS DRAWING CARTOONS, TOO...
Sorry, Mr. Callahan, we don't cash "Hustler" checks here.
FEMINIST BANK OF CALI
L.F.P.

BUT SOON WELFARE
CAUGHT UP WITH ME,
MADE ME PAY BACK
ALL THE MONEY I'D
MADE CARTOONING...

NOW, I'M WORKING OUT
A PLAN WITH WELFARE BY WHICH
I'LL BE ALLOWED TO KEEP A
PORTION OF THE MONEY I
MAKE CARTOONING.
   I STILL GET DEPRESSED
ABOUT MY SITUATION, BUT
ADRIENNE SOOTHES ME WITH
BIBLE VERSES...

ORAL SEX SLIME MUTANT

I'm downtown. I'm self-conscious. I'm driving as fast as I can. Everyone is looking at me. Goddam them! I should never have left the house.

This morning I woke up with a huge fever blister on my lip. I look like the oral sex slime mutant from Sewer Z. I got it from prolonged exposure to the 100-degree heat of two days ago, though looking at it, you would guess I'd spent three weeks chained to a gay urinal.

Thirty thousand dollars of psychotherapy and self-image building down the toilet. I've barely got the courage to look in the mirror much less into the faces of people. And the way they stare at it! It's unbelievable. I try to avoid the public by traveling through alleys and side streets. I know what thoughts people have when they see someone with a bad cold sore. "Poor herpes-ridden wretch!!" (At least people may be inclined to see me as a sexual being instead of an asexual cripple!)

The more I hide my infected face from the strangers who pass me by (who are aware that I am hiding a giant cold sore simply by the way I force my face in an opposite direction), the more monstrous I imagine my deformity.

"Callahan! Callahan!"

Dear God, who could be calling to me! Please, God, make them stop!

"Callahan! John Callahan!"

I hear the hysterical female voices coming closer and closer from behind. Bitch! Bitch! Why can't you give up?! There is nowhere for me to turn off on this busy downtown street! I'm trapped like a rat!

"Callahan! John Callahan!!"

My cold sore is growing bigger! I can see it in the faces of the oncoming people. They know it's the world's worst and largest cold sore and they cannot hide it in their eyes. Faster and faster I push the wheelchair.

"Callahan!! Callahan!!"

Now everyone is aware of what's going on. Now all of them know that I have the most enormous cold sore in all of medical science and I'm only trying to escape this persistent female who is trying to stop me to say hello. Oh, my God! The crosswalk light is turning red! I can't turn a corner because there's sidewalk construction on both right and left!

"Callahan!!!"

I'm trapped, I'm slowing my chair to a stop for the light.

"Callahan. Hi, Callahan!"

Slowly, my heart pounding, trapped, controlled and defeated, I turn my deformed countenance toward the direction of the voice that has hounded me—humiliated me! Expecting to see a girl's face smiling from a car window, I'm horrified to see the face is smiling from one of a hundred windows of a Greyhound bus.

"Callahan, Callahan!! Remember me? I met you ten years ago. . . . I used to pet your cat. . . . Hey, what's wrong with your lip? . . ."

"Bermuda Triangle shorts"

CALLAHAN

Here is a piece that I definitely would have risked my reputation on. Imagine my disillusionment when it received enough rejection slips to wallpaper a mansion with.

A NUCLEAR CHRISTMAS

'Twas a nuclear Christmas
when all through the shelter,
every creature was glowing
and ran helter skelter.

The stockings were hung
on the wall with precision,
in hopes that the mutant
would bring some provisions.

The children were nestled
all snug 'neath the floor,
in hopes of avoiding
a fourth World War.

And Momma in her kerchief,
and I in my cap,
slouched in the corner
with our heads in our laps.

When up on the street
There arose such a clatter,
I sprang from the floor
losing control of my bladder.

Then what to my wondering eyes
I should spy
but a two-headed man
with eight arms and six eyes.

Only one leg he had
And his skin was translucent,
I knew in a moment
it must be the mutant.

In the fallout he called out
I could hear him complaining,
"It's cold and it's lonely,
and this acid keeps raining.

"My eyes they are blinded
and I'm losing my hair,
my right leg is aching,
and my left leg's not there.

"I've seventeen ears,
and more that keep growing,
the amount I'll end up with,
there's no way of knowing.

"My elves aren't themselves
and my reindeer are history,
how I manage alone
is an absolute mystery.

"Yet I continue to work
with care and devotion,
for the few scattered souls
who survived the explosion."

With that he was silent,
and he stopped all his flapping.
From under the stairs,
I could hear his canes tapping.

My wife was disgusted,
by something I said,
when an ear dropped off
of one of his heads.

A bundle of things
he had flung on his back,
canned goods I think,
lead-lined at that.

With his noses like roses
he was not unattractive.
His cheeks were like cherries—
he was radioactive!

He'd a tumor on his back,
the size of a boulder.
A ninth arm was growing
from out of his shoulder.

He was bloated and gray
like a cancerous boar,
as wheezing and coughing,
he dropped to the floor.

A seizure now gripped him,
I saw with alarm.
I was wholly convinced
he was buying the farm.

When he pulled himself up
with repeated tries,
and filled all the stockings
with food and supplies

And laying a finger,
to the side of his nose,
it fell off his face
as up the stairway he rose.

And I heard him exclaim,
as I wakened my wife,
"A nuclear Christmas to all,
And to all a half-life."

AFTERWORD

I just got back yesterday from San Francisco where I went to visit Robin Williams. I met Debbie Levin there and we all worked to tie up the contract with Robin. I still can't get over the fact that Robin Williams purchased my life story as an option for a movie. His wife, Marsha, will be producing it, as she did *Mrs. Doubtfire,* and Robin will be playing me! (I'm still not sure how he will be able to hold still long enough to play a paralytic!)

Anyway, I got to hang around Robin on the set of a movie he was shooting and go to dinner with him and his wife. I humiliated myself by flinging my arm carelessly and knocking over a tray full of food from the waiter's hand, spilling food and sauce all over Robin's assistant. Everyone tried to make me feel better about my fopaw. (Robin even slipped into a frenetic "Mork" imitation, which disturbed everyone except me.) I was despondent. I tried to forget the incident, and even managed a weak smile, but I couldn't forgive my own stupidity. I knew Robin was secretly thinking, "That clumsy wretch! He should be locked up in a home! I can't possibly play his character in a movie! I've heard freaks are uncoordinated but this Callahan guy is beyond belief!!"

So it wasn't enough for me to mortify myself in front of Dylan, but the great loving spirit of the Universe saw fit to let me experience the pain all over again with Robin Williams.

I'm safe at home in Portland again! The rain is somehow comforting now. I'm getting used to it after all these years, I guess. But it depresses the shit out of most women up here. Eight out of ten are on Prozac.

But the rain makes me feel more creative. I've always vowed that one day I'd leave this soaked hellhole behind for a sunnier place! But as the years have passed, I've gotten more honest about it. I'd feel awkward in a sunny place like L.A. or Miami. I'd feel like a big fat paralyzed pink-skinned pig. In a sunnier place I cannot cover my pinkness and fatness with lots of baggy, dark clothing. I've decided to hang around and try my hand at writing a novel. Maybe a tragic love yarn or something. First off, I must take the wiener dog to the animal clinic, where I have a crush on a certain female veterinarian. I keep taking the dog into the clinic every few months with various vague complaints so that I can be near this lady. On the last visit something regrettable happened, of course. When Dr. Harris inserted the thermometer into the dog's rectum, I *winked* at her (not the dog—the vet!). She scowled disapprovingly at me and rolled back her eyes in disgust. I scooped up the dog, paid the bill, took the cab home, and here I sit waiting for the Muses to inspire me.

Do not judge me too harshly as you consume the last paltry words I scrawl here. I am but a simple cartoonist and do not know how to write a proper ending to a book. Sorry . . . ,

J.C.